What to do if your Ch

WHAT TO DO IF
YOUR CHILD CAN'T READ

Lyn Murray

Constable · London

First published in Great Britain 1999
by Constable and Company Limited,
3 The Lanchesters,
162 Fulham Palace Road,
London W6 9ER
Copyright © 1999 Lyn Murray
The right of Lyn Murray to be identified as the author
of this work has been asserted by her in accordance with
the Copyright, Designs and Patents Act 1988
ISBN 0 094 78270 9

Set in Linotron Sabon 11pt by
Rowland Phototypesetting Limited
Printed in Great Britain by
St Edmundsbury Press Ltd,
both of Bury St Edmunds, Suffolk

A CIP catalogue record for this book
is available from the British Library

Contents

Preface

Many young people who are involved in criminal behaviour can't read effectively. Their criminal behaviour is, of course, not the cause of the inability to read; but it is to a great extent the result of it. They have spent years in our educational system feeling increasingly excluded from what is going on around them in the classroom. They can't tackle course books, they can't read books and magazines comfortably and they feel acutely aware of their own incapacity. Because of their reading difficulties most have always felt to a greater or lesser extent shut out from the lives of other people of their own age. Some fall in with people who exploit them and some get into crime simply because they are bored and have serious financial problems because they are unable to achieve the qualifications that would make them eligible for the jobs they want.

Every year our schools get the maximum possible publicity for their exam successes. But this high-flyer culture leaves those children who fail their exams feeling even more devastated and inadequate. At present, 50,000 teenagers leave school without any qualifications each year and in 1998 the number of GCSE entries that did not merit even the lowest of the eight grades (bearing in mind that grades A–C are demanded by most employers and colleges) rose to 120,000, an increase of more than fifty per cent on the previous year.

Most young people who fail in school do so because they can't read effectively. Their reading skills are so poor that they feel uncomfortable even trying to read and although they often have lively minds their efforts to learn are frustrated by their inability to collect written information and interpret it clearly for all to see. Many feel so despondent that they decide that they just 'don't read' and reject lessons that rely on print out of hand.

Children have the basic right to be taught how to read and write, and the National Literacy Strategy is a step in the right direction, setting out structured teaching objectives for reading and using language in primary schools as well as promoting reading throughout a child's school career. But it is not the New Jerusalem. Children still require individual attention and learning which is geared to their own particular tastes and requirements. Schools need greater resources together with teachers who don't feel so tired or overworked that they can't project their enthusiasm for reading and learning. Children must be valued and guided to success in whatever they want to achieve. They need to grow in confidence and perseverance, to learn how to work with others and organise their own lives, but this is made so much more difficult if they aren't given the means to become skilled readers.

Reports suggest that children who have moved up through primary school without becoming confident about their reading skills don't find the extra reading time they are given under the guidelines of the literacy strategy either helpful or fulfilling. They feel stupid and isolated as they flip through books aimlessly, or cause trouble to other readers because they feel left out. Some are faced with the prospect of taking exams whose question papers they may not even be capable of deciphering and they are terrified of being seen to fail. Literacy is everything; if a child can't fully understand what she is reading she is at an immediate disadvantage, will swiftly become disenchanted with education and frequently will simply stop trying.

If your child is finding reading a trial rather than a source of fun and enjoyment she needs help, time and understanding. This book is designed to help you to help her, whether she has just started school and seems unsure about books or is facing secondary education without the ability to read and understand exam work. It will enable you to get the best possible help for your child in school as well as showing you ways to work with her at home to overcome her reading difficulties.

Children are usually the first to be aware that they are not mastering a skill as fast as their friends. Once they start to feel uneasy about their ability to read they become stressed and angry, and this spills over into family life. Sadly, there are no magic formulae: they will have to be taught with patience, method and an ability to communicate enthusiasm. They won't learn to read by osmosis without mastering the conventions of language, and they need to be shown what fun written words can be and how useful they are. Your positive help and attention is vital. I hope this book will guide you into helping your child to read happily and confidently so that books become a pleasure for you both.

Introduction

Reading difficulties can make any child start to feel a failure. Everyone seems to be moving on happily, in a reading world that she somehow can't find her way into. Children who don't learn to read in class can start to feel as if they are trapped behind a glass door, watching their friends pass through. This sense of isolation is made stronger by the fact that the child doesn't know where she is going wrong. Even very young children get distressed if they can't do something others seem to find easy. As any parent of a child who has been through this experience knows, a child who is unhappy at school can make life hell for everyone who cares for her. Hurt and frustrated children behave badly – and so the spiral begins.

At present some of our children are being thrown away by our educational system. Schools, ever conscious of their need to produce excellent exam results, often feel the need to concentrate on those children who don't experience difficulties in reading and writing, and have a realistic chance of passing exams without having to be given an educational programme catering for their own special needs and abilities. Children who understandably feel left out and discounted stop trying, and either become apathetic and resigned to failure or start to cause trouble. Without being given the means to learn in a way suited to their capabilities, some children don't have a hope of going into the exam room with the same opportunities as others in their class. Poor readers make simple mistakes misreading questions, and so can even fail those practical subjects which they would have a good chance of passing if only they had more confidence and better reading ability.

Anyone who has had to invigilate in an exam room where some of the students sit staring blankly until they are allowed to leave cannot help but realise that we are just torturing children who can't cope with the exam system. They leave school branded as failures because, often through poor literacy and lack of basic learning and organisation skills, they don't understand how to tackle exams. All these students have strengths and abilities that are not being built on. They don't fit into the mould of success that is mapped out, they are not book learners and they aren't shown any other ways to succeed. The rise in the number of students leaving secondary education with no GCSEs must not be allowed to continue; education must give all children the means to learn everything that they want and need to know, and this must start by spending all the time and money necessary to give them the skill to read – something that is inevitably the key.

By explaining reading issues that worry many parents this book offers advice to anyone who wants to know how to stop the spiral in its tracks. One of the most important things to remember is never to let your children feel that reading is something that they aren't going to master effectively – a child who expects to fail often stops trying to succeed. She can do it and, with time and practice, she will. The aim of this book is to help children of any age who find reading a barrier to learning – from five-year-olds in need of a little loving help and encouragement, to fourteen-year-olds who could face failing practical GCSEs simply because they cannot read and interpret questions successfully. Not only does it show you how you can help your child to read at home, but it also offers guidance about how the educational system in the UK works, and what you can do to make sure that it works for your child's benefit is she is having difficulty with reading. It will take you through the practical and emotional reasons why your child may be having problems with reading, and show you how to help in a way that shouldn't cause undue stress to you or your family.

1

How Children Learn to Read

Teaching a child to read is like searching for a light switch in a dark room. Sometimes it is quick and easy but sometimes it takes a deal of time and trouble. If your child finds reading a problem rather than a pleasure, look for a reason and do everything you can to help him win through. Once you have exhausted the probable without success start looking at the improbable and never give up. No matter how much effort it takes, learning to read effectively switches on a light that no child would ever want switched off again.

If reading is a big part of your life it can come as a real shock if your child doesn't grasp books with the same enthusiasm. You have spent years reading to your child and telling him stories. He has been shown how books work and how enjoyable they can be. Quite understandably, most parents expect and hope that their child will learn from their example and will quickly come to share in their enthusiasm. It is so difficult not to surreptitiously compare your child's progress with that of another, to feel anxious that a friend's child seems so much more advanced even though he is the same age as your own. But every child is different and all children are complicated in their way. Of course they need to be taught to read in a structured and skilled way; but their own predispositions will influence how they will learn most successfully.

Reading is arguably the most important skill that your child will ever learn. If a child learns to read effectively in his first years at school he is able to use that knowledge throughout his school life. If he can't learn to read, much of what is being taught to him in the classroom will remain a mystery. Your help and your confidence in his ability to succeed is vital, remember that he is an incomparable person who needs support and acclaim rather than criticism and pressure.

One thing that most parents and teachers learn from bitter experience is that, in general, boys and girls have different and distinct likes and dislikes. Women and girls are generally more fluent conversationalists, with minds which tend to be more active in the regions that concern emotions. Men and boys are stronger on spatial tasks and physical activity. Although many parents struggle to bring up male and female children the same way in order to give them the maximum choices in life, boys and girls behave differently in many ways. As they grow up, boys will tend towards competitive games – while girls will tend to co-operate in playtime activities. Almost every playground has its male team rivalries and enclaves of girls either deep in conversation or taken up with arguments about friendship groups. Just as boys and girls often show different preferences for toys and activities, they usually choose different role models from whom to learn, and different books to learn with. No matter how hard one tries to avoid it, the classic stereotypes are based on some facts that cannot be ignored. While boys and girls like many of the same books, some do make what could be regarded as very sexist choices, and you need to accept and accommodate these preferences. Although the idea of it may make many concerned parents cringe, young girls tend to enjoy reading about fabulous 'Barbie' life-styles, fairies and animals. But if boys are asked to read about princesses and ponies they are likely to make their excuses and leave. Children are obviously attracted to reading books that they find appealing and if you want them to settle happily into reading it's important to offer them books that they will positively want to read. If you are really keen not to offer your child sexually stereotyped books, both boys and girls flourish on books that make them laugh and where everyone tries to puzzle out the punchline.

When you are working with your child to help ease him into independent reading, accept his individual nature and work with it to bring about the best possible outcome. One-parent families can provide as effective an education and home life as any other type of family group; but the child who sees only a parent of the opposite sex reading may come to consider it something for him or her alone to enjoy. Boys will often respond better to male teachers; however, in first schools male teachers are a rarity. If you are a single mother bringing up a boy, or a single father bringing up a girl, you may need to acknowledge that when it comes to reading, a positive role model of the opposite gender could help. If a caring and patient friend, or family member, shows a child how much he or she enjoys reading, that can act as a powerful spur to getting your boy or girl into reading happily.

When a child is not learning to read successfully, the finger inevitably points to the system which educates him. Most parents – and teachers – believe that they could run education more effectively; doubtless, many of them are right. Express your views and become involved with your child's school, but remember that no school can be run successfully without an element of compromise. If you feel that teaching is inad-equate, do try to find a subtle, non-confrontational way of expressing your fears. Being actively forthright with your child's teacher may make you feel better, but it can be deeply embarrassing for your child. Remember, you are just a visitor, but your child has to meet that person every day.

Work with the school to help them discover how your child will learn best. Your child's teacher wants her or him to be happy and successful in class almost as much as you do. It is not a profession in which you can remain detached; thirty or more children, each with a complicated character, are growing and developing in front of you every school-day. Nine times out of ten, you will find that a teacher will want the same for your child as you do – happiness and success.

A keen awareness of the differences between the personalities of individual children is important and no two children start school with the same experience. Some will be able to read quite independently, while others have never picked up a book. Your child's teacher may have to teach more than thirty very different children each with particular needs and idiosyncrasies. The teacher, by necessity has to use a mixture of various structured teaching methods in order to please most of the people most of the time.

Although such teaching methods are often shrouded in jargon, they are all basically simple and straightforward, and once you have grasped the essentials you will be able to make use of them at home. When you are working towards reading with your child you will gradually find that he seems happiest with one or two teaching styles. Work with these – after all, any child will learn faster and more effectively if he feels relaxed and confident. You don't need to find ways of teaching a broad range of children, you are teaching a child whom no one knows better than you do. Find the way he enjoys learning best and work within that.

The three most commonly used methods of teaching children to read are phonics, 'look and say', and the 'language/ real book' approach. In my view, the most fundamental and effective is phonics – the sounds and spellings of individual and groups of letters within words. The most obvious starting point when teaching a child to read is to make sure he has a good knowledge of the alphabet. But a child needs to understand not simply the sounds of individual letters within the alphabet, but also the sounds each letter is most likely to make within a word. Although the alphabet consists of only twenty-six letters, the number of phonemes (basic sound units) in the English language means that in total the child learning to read must master over forty individual and distinct sounds. As well as being able to distinguish one heard phoneme from another he needs to be able to recognise these same sounds when they are represented by written letters. All letters, and groups of letters, have sounds that can be learned and used to build up the words that are to be read. Words, like other puzzles, can be worked out by considering their separate elements, by taking them apart and putting them together.

Some children give the impression that they can memorise every word they see almost photographically. They begin to read confidently almost on sight; but without the scaffolding of phonics to build on remembering an increasingly broad range of words becomes a strain. Many children are excellent detectives – they can work out words because they are reading a very predictable text. But ultimately this can be the reading equivalent of using a trapeze without a safety net – impressive to watch, but likely to end in trouble.

In my experience, some of the children who have been assumed by parents (and sometimes teachers) to be dyslexic are instead children who have failed to acquire good reading skills, for the simple reason that they have been badly taught. By ignoring phonic rules, their teachers place these children in the position of having to learn to read by remembering words as individual images or shapes, without component parts. Many children find this approach virtually impossible. These children need to be shown the means of building up and deciphering words from the clues inherent within each word, rather than having to rely on clues they encounter in the context of the story, or in the pictures that accompany the words.

Clues, then, can help you to read – but you need a method of deciphering them, or their help is erratic to say the least. One important argument for the use of phonics is that while, for various reasons, boys learn to read by most methods slightly less readily than girls, when intensive phonics are used to help trigger reading, both sexes achieve the same good level of success.

One major problem with phonics is that they are extremely difficult to teach in an entertaining and informative way; taught badly, they are liable to turn more children away from reading than towards it. It is essential that they are taught cheerfully and well, by someone who clearly finds the process of reading exciting. Hopefully, this will be your child's teacher. Realistically, it could well be down to you and one of the aims of this book is to outline interesting ways of teaching this essential part of reading. Learning the correspondence between written letters and groups of letters (graphemes) and the units of sound that they make (phonemes) is always difficult. A useful section on phonemes and phonetics is included in the Appendix, along with games and exercises for you to use with your child.

English spelling is often illogical and most of the basic two hundred key words most commonly used in English have irregular spelling patterns which can't be worked out easily using phonics. The 'Look-and-Say' method involves learning to recognise words on sight. Its importance becomes much

more significant when we realise that more than half of everything we read is composed of a basic one hundred words (see
Appendix for the complete list). These simple, everyday words
need to be learned until they are read automatically and
quickly, with no hesitation. Once children can do this, they
will feel confident to tackle most text and work out those
words they don't understand. Repetition of basic words is at
the core of most popular reading schemes.

In order to form an effective reading scheme, the 'Look-
and-Say' form of teaching should work hand in hand with
the phonics method. The more phonics a child recognises,
the easier he will find it is to read and spell. Many children
can pick up letter/sound combinations very quickly; it is
essential to keep their interest by moving with them. But it
is important to remember that while phonics are undoubtedly
a remarkably effective help with reading, the English language
can be very illogical – try reading 'enough' by sounding it
out – and the need for other reading schemes working in
conjunction with phonics becomes clear.

The 'real book', or 'whole language' approach to reading
was, until recently, more popular with many teachers than
the phonic method. The idea behind it is that children should
become involved in reading by concentrating on remembering
the words they see, and predicting new words within the
context of the story. 'Real books' are story and picture books
– not books specifically designed solely to form part of a
phonic reading scheme. When reading with the child, a
teacher will point out letters and words, and discuss the content of the book. It is important to support this by doing the
same when the child brings the reading book home. The
advantage of the 'real book' method is that children can
choose their own books and move forward at their own pace.
Some children love this approach, as they seem to remember

the shape and structure of words on sight; however, many others find such immediate confrontation with reading daunting. There is nothing wrong with the 'real book' method for children it suits, but there is no point in insisting on using this method for children it does not. They need the structure of phonics to give them something to build on.

We have seen the three fundamental methods of teaching reading outlined in brief. But how can you help, if your child has started school and just doesn't seem to be taking to reading happily? One of the most important things to remember is that if you are obviously worried, this will in turn worry your child. Most children who find difficulties when they begin to learn to read at school usually have trouble with settling down, concentrating and remembering – skills that, until full-time school, they have seldom needed to practise. They just haven't learned how to learn. All these problems can be solved with time, tolerance, patience and ingenuity. As with any difficult situation, if the answer seems impossible to discover, it usually helps to approach the problem differently, to find a solution by seeing things from every point of view.

Here is an example from my own experience as a primary teacher.

Cathy regularly came home with a reading book, and a few words or sounds to learn. At first she was excited by the whole idea of joining in with her friends and being able to read herself; but she gradually became more and more resentful when her parents asked her what she had learned. Although at first she had tried very hard to keep the words and letters she had been expected to learn in her head, she just wasn't remembering them from one day to the next and began to feel disenchanted. Even mastering the basic sounds of the alphabet was a bit of a problem. She began to feel unsure of herself and her ability to cope, and turned away from reading altogether.

Children like Cathy need to have their confidence raised and maintained. To be told that their achievements – which might seem slight to an adult – are all brilliant and worthwhile in their own right. Every method of teaching reading relies to a great extent on remembering what is seen and heard. Eventually, with practice, most people can remember and recognise thousands of words so easily that they can read non-technical books at a rate of around three hundred words a minute, without any conscious effort. But reading anything full of words you can't recognise or understand inevitably leads to a sense of isolation and boredom. Remember, when your child is beginning to read nearly every word is indecipherable. Praise is never wasted.

As well as praise, Cathy needed to be given strategies and practice to help her to learn and recall what she learned. When they are starting to read, children have to remember letter shapes and sounds, and playing alphabet games together is frequently a very good beginning. In Cathy's case, her family tried to use old ABC books to rekindle her interest. In fact, these well-intentioned attempts were counterproductive – Cathy dismissed the books as 'for babies' and was embarrassed to be associated with them. It rapidly developed into what appeared to be an insurmountable problem, which was eventually solved by approaching it from another direction. Cathy was only prepared to consider books she felt would be appropriate for her age, but she needed to learn alphabet basics. She rejected every book her parents found until they suggested that she might like to produce her very own alphabet book – for her younger brother to use.

Like most young children, Cathy thrived upon a challenge,

especially one she felt confident she might win. Her brother loved food so, using a small blank exercise book, and with the help of her family close at hand, she made an ABC of all her brother's favourite foods. Every letter stood for something. Admittedly, this led to some dubious culinary decisions – such as the blood-curdling Z for Zebra. Carefully, Cathy illustrated the book with her own drawings and pictures cut from magazines. Her brother was delighted, and asked his sister to read the book over and over again. After several weeks of reading the book to her brother every night, Cathy herself knew all the alphabet sounds which had been troubling her – without even realising she had learned them. Teaching by stealth can be very effective.

Like Cathy, many children find remembering the sound of a letter, and relating it to the words that begin with it, extremely difficult. Such difficulties mean that a child can easily panic but these initial fears can often be overcome by the use of simple games which are both informative and fun. Gradually, the link between the letter and the sound it makes becomes a familiar everyday activity and just an ordinary part of life. Children, like adults, remember funny things; so try inventing alliterative sentences which make them laugh. You might feel ridiculous reciting 'jumping Jennifer juggles jelly', but your child will love every word and remember clearly the sound that j makes in a word. Once this game becomes too easy, try moving, with your child, through the alphabet – asking him, as Cathy was asked, to name food, or other items, in alphabetical order. The old game of everyone naming something that begins with the same letter remains constantly amusing and effective. Running through the alphabet – A for apple, B for banana, each person coming up with a fruit (or anything else!) beginning with the next consecutive letter – teaches children the alphabet and lays the foundation for a good knowledge of alphabetical order, something which can only be learned by repetition.

Ideally, writing down the words thrown up from these games and reading them through together can be hugely enjoyable, both for child and parent. But writing isn't always necessary. One big advantage of these games is that they can be played while you are concentrating on other things. You can play them with your child in the car, when you are walking, or working around your home. The more fun he has practising the more automatic his knowledge of alphabet sounds will become. If your child starts to be bored or disheartened, it's best to stop. But be warned – when children get the hang of these games, they can be very eager to play.

Some children, like Cathy, become frightened of attempting to read because they find it overly daunting. Others reject reading simply because they fail to see the point in it. Tom, for example, failed to make much headway in class for the obvious reason that he had absolutely no interest in books. Like most little boys, he enjoyed running, playing and making things – however, he would only pick up a book when he wanted to use it as part of a game. Once more, the solution came not in repeating old rules and lessons over again, but in approaching the problem from a different position.

Tom's mother and his teacher were both concerned to create a way for him to discover writing without feeling he was forced to sit down and read a book. Fortunately, they realised that words were all around them – on packages, on toys and on signs. The next time Tom's mother went into town with him, she began to gently introduce the idea of writing, pointing out the many signs everywhere they went and asking if he could tell what they said. When they looked at toys together, for example, Tom was expected to attempt to decipher what was inside their boxes. Sometimes he would make wild, ludicrous guesses which provoked both mother and son into fits of laughter; sometimes he would be right. On a good day, such journeys were extremely enjoyable for the pair, and every word learned added to Tom's confidence and interest.

At school, Tom had been learning basic phonics with very little interest but when his mother encouraged him to read by breaking down words into their component parts, writing acquired new meaning for him. By asking Tom to read about things which he found interesting and important, his mother taught him to see the use of reading for him. They read through instruction leaflets for toys and computer games together, and used television listings to find out when favourite programmes would be on. Although he was still not particularly interested in books – reading them only when asked – a growing awareness of the importance and relevance that writing and reading had to his everyday life meant that he could, at least, see the value of understanding words and learning to read them.

This highlights an important point. Even if you love books, there is actually no imperative reason why your children should. Beyond school, the crucial value of reading is indeed for deciphering mundane things like instruction leaflets and the TV guide.

It is not only boys who fail to see the purpose of reading – although the reasons given by girls are often extremely difficult. Amy and Louise had been best friends since playgroup, and spent most of their days playing contentedly together. Although they would join in whole-class reading sessions happily, they saw little purpose in reading alone, preferring to enjoy one another's company. They would fight for the chance to work together, but were totally unwilling to choose books individually. Teaching them to read by the traditional methods was totally unsuccessful; again, they only decided to learn when the rules were made to suit them.

Their closeness was the major factor in Amy's and Louise's school lives, so their teacher decided to exploit it by asking them to work together at preparing a shop in the corner of the classroom. Cardboard boxes were soon covered with labels and signs, as both children became progressively more involved in the fantasy. Soon, they were arriving at school with leaflets, magazines and posters provided by their local superstore – eager to know and understand the meaning of any writing they could find about shops and shopping.

This was not, of course, an ideal solution; both children remained, for the time being, uninterested in books. But at least the shop scenario had been realistically devised to appeal to their interests and inspire them with a desire to learn. Amy's and Louise's interest in books could not be forced; their reluctance to read had to be accepted and the two children taught to learn on their own terms. The solution was not perfect, but it was a positive and significant move forward, enabling the children to obtain both confidence and an awareness of the relevance of the world of reading to themselves. This sense of confidence was increased by the fact that many other children envied their position as class shopkeepers. Amy and Louise now felt they were an important part of the class – their social circle widened and they always had plenty to discuss. Although their friendship remained strong, they found themselves increasingly involved in the class as a whole, and in class lessons.

The lesson learned by the example of Amy and Louise may be applied to many cases. Children love role-play and it can be a great way to get them interested in reading. If your child enjoys these games, try helping him to make the sort of store which he most enjoys visiting. Cardboard box post offices, for example, can easily be filled with old leaflets and letters – fun to play with and an excellent way to get your child to read. Try to make sure that any role-play at home involves other children and, if you have the time, remember that children love 'selling' items in their shop to adults – although you may not always get what you ask for!

As well as getting a child to read, role-playing can often help to build confidence. Setting up a mock hospital, dentist or school can be great fun to children, and it also helps them to feel more in control if they are anticipating a visit. Help them to make simple signs – 'open' and 'closed', 'pull' and 'push' – and read them together wherever you see them. Role-playing is not just an effective way to teach word recognition; it can also teach children how to behave in everyday situations. As we have seen, some children have trouble with reading because they would rather be physically active. If this is the case, accept it and work with it. Always help a child to read and write whatever he wishes. Many children who take a dismissive approach to reading are more content with painting and art than with writing or reading. In such situations, encourage your child to paint a picture and explain what it means to you; then, with his agreement, write his explanation beneath the picture. A picture of his day out can in this way become a very memorable and personal illustrated short story. Putting the picture before the story is often the best way to get children to think about what they have been doing and thinking about. Some children can talk about what they see – even if they have completed that picture themselves – but not have the confidence to tell a story 'from cold'. Such simple methods, stressing the relevance of writing to the child's own life, are almost always an easy encouragement towards reading success.

Learning relies very much on motivation. Watch your child

playing and pick up on what interests him. Help him to use photos and pictures to tell about a trip, make up board games, get toys to write to each other. Encourage your child to use words, both written and spoken, as part of his games.

Some children will always find it difficult to sit calmly and settle to reading and, as we have seen, in these cases it is often best to attempt to introduce reading into their own personal activities. While this technique will help to teach even the least willing, it often remains difficult to persuade children that sitting quietly, even to read, can be fun or even that it can be tolerated. It is important to remember that until full-time school begins most children have had no need to spend time in studied concentration – no wonder, then, that it frequently seems alien and unnatural.

If your child is finding settling to read at school difficult, try mimicking school conditions when he is at home. This needs to be done subtly for the obvious reason that any child ordered to sit still at home will almost certainly feel resentful and imprisoned. Try finding some time, after a meal, when both you and your child are calm and relaxed. Then, making sure that all of his toys have been put away, relax, sit down, and start to read a book yourself. The fact that you are obviously finding what you are reading far more entertaining than paying attention to him will soon make your child start to feel jealous and irritable. Basically, he will want some of what you're having, to participate in the activity that you are obviously finding so enjoyable. At this point, give your child a book of his own so that he can read quietly alongside you. If such tactics are used regularly, a child will often quickly absorb the habit of quietly reading a book.

Some educationalists and newspapers can inspire feelings of guilt for those of us even owning a television. Obviously, using the television as a constant baby-sitter is to be avoided;

but selective viewing can help to bring children into the sequence and magic of stories. Favourite programmes can also serve as a way of helping children to sit quietly and concentrate on a story – just as they should in their school studies. Children love to watch the same video repeatedly, predicting the actions of the characters before they occur. This repetition will probably drive the other members of your family to fury; but persevere – it can encourage children to concentrate and follow the structure of a story. If you can stand it, try asking them what happens next in the plot, before it arrives and later ask them to think about what they have watched and retell the story to you.

Most young children develop a passion for characters they see in films and on television. They can seem very real to the children, who love to read about them. Many who have appeared very lukewarm about their reading books at school can become spectacularly keen to read about their latest TV icon. It is well worthwhile making sure that you have books about your child's favourite film or television characters so that you can capture his motivation to read about them while it lasts. Even those who are naturally disinclined to settle will watch television calmly if you can spend the time to watch it with them, and this can be a useful first step towards making your child a reader. Neither of you needs to watch passively – indeed, it is often better to talk about the story, to call out the programme title together and to share your enjoyment. Even if you cannot spend the time to sit with him as much as you would like, television can be useful as well as amusing. Simply by sitting alone watching a favourite video, a child is learning both to concentrate on and analyse the beginning, middle and end of a story.

Television can give children a keen appetite for tales, rhymes and characters, and serve as a valuable guide for those who are otherwise uninterested in reading. If your child does build up a special interest in a particular character or programme, try never to complain. When there are no written stories available concerning that character or programme, encourage your child to tell you stories about them which you can write and he can illustrate. When you are helping a child to read, any progress you make is positively and permanently won.

Before a child starts to read, it helps if he has already had happy experiences of stories, songs and rhymes. Those children fortunate enough to have been sung to regularly, and to have heard stories and rhymes from a very early age, often come to link these positive early memories to the idea of learning about words. Remembering and repeating nursery rhymes helps to develop concentration and memory – it can also serve to boost confidence. Studies have suggested that children who can recognise rhyme at the age of three are more likely to become successful readers at the age of six.

Learning rhyme is a valuable tool in word recognition; it is easier to remember and predict the sounds in a rhyme than it is in almost all prose stories, and as we have seen, memory and prediction are essential aspects of the good reader. Rhyme also brings home that words have endings as well as beginnings and that every part of every word is important. Children particularly enjoy making up insulting rhymes about their friends and family – so, if you think you can take it, have a go. Funny rhymes will always be appreciated more than bland ones, and remember – the quality of the poetry is not important, these are just ways of playing, and growing familiar with words. As with the word game ideas outlined earlier in this chapter, they may be played even when you are actively involved in other tasks. Children often like to have the rhymes they have invented written down so that you can read them together over again. Rhyming is a brilliant way to practise phonics – and it can be a lot of fun.

Simple strategies can, hopefully, encourage most children towards reading both on their own and as part of a group during their first years at school. But if your child still seems eager to avoid reading at all costs, trust your instincts. If you feel that he has a problem, get help. Check with experts that your child can see and hear normally. Visually tackling text, and being able to discriminate between letters and words which are often superficially very similar, obviously requires a good level of eyesight. Hearing is no less vital – in learning to read, it is essential that a child can hear and distinguish the often subtle variations between phonemes. On a less complex level, it is easy for a hearing-impaired child to confuse one word read by a teacher or parent for another. I can clearly remember reading the phrase 'the trumpeter played with a flourish' to one class, only to find a child harbouring the conviction that I had actually said 'the trumpeter played with a florist'. Although this was undoubtedly the more interesting version of the story, it also led to a great deal of confusion.

It is important to realise that young children are often unaware that their senses are in any way different from those of other people. Children might regard their vision or hearing as perfectly efficient for running, playing, talking and painting, not understanding the concentration required for writing and reading. Children who seem to their friends and family to have normal hearing often find the classroom a confusing place, if they have poor auditory discrimination for certain sounds. When so much in reading and writing depends upon the ability to distinguish between sounds and letters which are sometimes very similar, it is little wonder that those with even a slight hearing or visual disability can find themselves dropping behind in class.

Here's another example from my own experience.

Claudia seemed to be taking to reading like a duck to water. She had always loved picture books and listening to stories, and was keen to be able to read for herself. At first, she came home with books that had just one line of simple words on each page. She remembered every word she learned, and tried to work out those she wasn't sure of from memory, use of phonics and the simple context clues in the story. But as she became a more skilled reader the books she was given became longer and Claudia seemed to be increasingly confused. While reading one line of text on a page was straightforward, a block of lines close together often seemed to be blurred and unclear. In class Claudia kept up well because she was quick for her age and she was seldom in the position of having to read a page crowded by many lines of words. But at home, where she enjoyed looking at books belonging to her elder brother and sister, her difficulty with pages crammed with text became increasingly apparent.

Claudia had always enjoyed snuggling up with one of her parents in the evening to read and be read to. It was during one of these times that her father first noticed the book she was trying to read upset her. He thought at first that the words were simply too difficult. But when he tried writing each sentence down to help her practise the words, Claudia's father was surprised to find she could read his large, printed writing easily. He watched her with her own reading books to see if he could notice where things were going wrong for Claudia. Gradually he observed that the sentences she was reading were becoming a confused jumble because she was picking up words from the writing above and below the line she was reading. With the increasingly small print that she was having to tackle in the more advanced story books, this problem became progressively worse.

Claudia's parents had never suspected that her eyesight was deficient in any way. She was alert, bright and happy, and had always been able to take an active part in school work and home life. But distinguishing one line of small print from another was something she hadn't tried to do before. Being a very able child, who enjoyed school, she had had few difficulties with her school work. When her problem was first discovered by her father, there had not been any circumstances in class which had meant that Claudia's problem had been one she could not disguise. By discovering it early, Claudia's father was able to solve his daughter's difficulties before they even began – reading glasses made each word and line far more clear and distinct, and Claudia's reading moved from strength to strength.

Another important and often overlooked practical reason for a barrier to reading is the basic fact that some children find being indoors, and restrained to study, deeply constricting. This is not a simple problem of merely failing to settle – such children are so physically active by nature that a normal classroom situation can make them feel both physically and mentally trapped. As we have seen, this problem can affect both sexes; however, it happens predominantly with boys, who are generally more eager to build physical strength than theoretical knowledge. Such children often feel tense in the classroom – as in the example of Jack.

Jack was an intelligent boy – curious, and interested in the world around him. Unlike his brother and two sisters, who had initially been reluctant to go to school, Jack, who loved the games of play-school, was eager to begin school life. In his first term, Jack attended only for the mornings, joining in with activities and making friends. However, difficulties began when he was expected to attend school full-time. Getting him to school became a hard feat every morning, fraught with tantrums and resistance. His teacher, too, was beginning to find Jack a strain on the classroom – he was constantly in trouble for refusing to sit and forever interrupting and wandering around. He persistently refused to join in in quiet reading and writing times, preferring to play with toys on his own. For Jack, the idea of learning to read had very little attraction, because he couldn't do it while he was running around.

A child who needs to learn through action is challenging even to teach alone, and it is inevitably stressful to teach such a child, in the manner he needs to be taught, within the framework of a large class. Necessarily, most teaching your child will be given in the classroom is aimed at the middle range of the class. Those who are ahead, or who suffer difficulties, are bound to feel marginalised to a greater or lesser extent.

Both Jack's mother and his teacher realised that he had a problem, which they had to work together to alleviate. The first, simple step was to make sure that Jack took far more exercise before, during and after school. His mother was lucky enough to be able to arrange for friends to take her other children to school. Free to concentrate on Jack, she had time to wake him earlier and spend some time playing with him in the park before lessons began. When he arrived at school, Jack was very grateful for the rest, and felt far less stressed about being expected to sit quietly through his lessons.

Ever since Jack had started school, he had been disinclined to read. Although he would enjoy choosing books, and studying them briefly, the process of sitting quietly and reading was quite alien to him. However, his teacher had noticed he was far more willing when reading with a class – playing along with the actions and enjoying the jokes with his friends. Exploiting this tendency, she allowed him to choose the books she read in class, on the condition that he was willing to sit in silence while all the children listened. Jack found enjoyment in choosing the stories he liked best and developed a fondness for those which involved a good deal of group activity, and his teacher, in turn, was rewarded with a happy class session.

After they had finished, she asked Jack to summarise the plot of the story in front of the class. His summaries were such a success that he was later encouraged to act out the story, with other children, in assembly. One of the unexpected bonuses was that Jack's ebullience influenced other, quieter children, who were encouraged by his lively good humour to join in the play.

Gradually, Jack's behaviour in class became easier to live with, and more productive both for himself and for those around him. He was never punished for minor misdemeanours by being kept in – his teacher knew that this only made matters worse, and his mother continued this method at home. Every effort was made to ensure that Jack was given exercise both at home and at school, that he ate regularly and was persuaded to go to sleep on time. Although reading was now far less of a problem at school, Jack was still unwilling to read silently at home, and the suggestion that he work on his reading book was often the cue for arguments and tantrums. Eventually, his family arrived at a reasonable solution; after he'd eaten, his older brothers would read with him, encouraging him to chime in those words he knew and understood throughout the story. In a few months, he was so skilled at this game that he could even read short stories to his brothers on his own. Jack was still only interested in books he found exciting, he enjoyed improbable adventures but was less than willing to read books chosen by other people. The problem wasn't solved completely but Jack was happier coping in class and the people around him were far less stressed.

No matter how well reading is taught at a school, if it doesn't engage your child's attention you will find you have a problem on your hands. Catch reading reluctance early and most difficulties can be deflated, if not entirely resolved, by the use of time, effort and a careful plan. Although this may seem hard, it will ultimately save you and your family considerable stress and strain. It is easier, after all, to arrive at school following a reasonably pleasant hour playing in the park with your child, than after another interminable breakfast-time tantrum.

Throughout this chapter, I have attempted to show a few easy ways of solving some of the key difficulties in getting your child to read. At the back of the book there are lists of common (key) words, rhymes and phonemes to base your word games around. If your child's behaviour hints at any physical difficulty, get expert assessment; if he just doesn't want to get down to reading exactly what you or his school wants him to read, try to engineer a compromise. If your child will only read books about television characters, about a favourite hobby, or with a friend, indulge him – the important thing is that he be motivated to read at all and that he enjoys it enough to keep on trying. If your child is only willing to read as part of a role-playing game, play with him. He is, after all, learning to read in his own way. A child will necessarily react against a situation in which he feels bullied, or bored; the obvious is true – a happy child makes for a successful child.

2

Reading at Home and at School

All children are unique, and all children develop their abilities
at different rates. Some children will, for example, begin to
read independently within the first year of full-time schooling;
others will necessarily need a little longer before they feel
confident enough to read independently. It is important not
to pressure your child too much – some children become so
nervous under pressure that this affects their ability to learn.
Judge the level of help that you need to give by asking both
teacher and child.

A reading scheme devised by Dame Marie Clay in New
Zealand – identifying and working to resolve a child's reading
difficulties by the age of six – has enabled the New Zealand
educational system to achieve a very high standard of literacy;
but (at the time of writing) most British schools do not offer
specialist help within mainstream schools for reading difficulties before a child reaches the age of seven. Classes are
generally larger and education can only be effectively managed with a formal 'common denominator' approach. In such
crowded conditions a child's individual reading difficulties
can be passed over even though the sense of confusion
experienced by a child with reading difficulties can lead to
acute problems from the very start. In an ideal world, there
is much to be said for attending to a child's learning problems

sympathetically and skilfully in the first year of schooling, rather than waiting until she has reached seven years of age. Children need to be offered sympathetic help and attention as soon as they feel the need for it; they will know they are struggling and want to be given the means to solve their own problems.

If, once your child has been tested negative for visual or aural disability, she continues to have reading difficulties, the primary causes are likely to be attitude and emotional stress, and deficiencies in the three major requirements of learning to read – a good knowledge of the phonic components of words, an ability to recognise keywords by sight, and a good capacity to detect unknown words in the context of their sentence or story. Most children have to feel comfortable with all three components before they can be fully at ease with the process of reading.

Through being away from school at a crucial time, or simply by not paying attention, children can lose out on essential basic learning. While many will remember easy single letters, some find it extremely difficult to understand the relation of letter groups to the sounds they make. Phonemes such as 'oa', or 'ea' – known as 'phonic blends' – are hard to learn and confusing to comprehend for the young child who has just been told that the individual letters within the combination both also hold their own phoneme. They understand the logic of making up words like c-a-t by building up single letter sounds; but words like clean or roam don't make the same kind of sense. They need to be learned from memory, and there are games at the end of the book to help with this.

When you listen to your child read, be sensitive and try to isolate where most of the difficulties lie. Read with her and look out for any signs that might indicate whether she has difficulty with basic sounds, with the beginnings or endings of words, or with letter groups. By all means keep helping her to practise and build upon her strong points to keep her confidence high; but you also need to discern the areas where she struggles to enable you to teach her where she is weakest. There is no need to watch her intensely, writing everything down – your child will be as unnerved by this behaviour as you would be, and undoubtedly less willing to work. If she stumbles frequently, talk to her about what she finds hardest. Most children are very realistic. They will ask for help if they are certain that you will still think that they are doing well and that you will help them to overcome their problems. Discuss what you have noticed with your child's teacher, and together you can work to plug the gaps. Often a child is thrown by some small teaching or home problem which may appear very simple, or even ridiculous, but remains crucial in teaching that child to read. Children have their own priorities, and tiny incidents can colour how they feel about far bigger things – as Lisa's parents discovered.

Lisa's first year at school was a happy one. She made friends, loved the activity and enjoyed reading sessions. But during the first term of her second year it became clear that she was no longer happy at school. She was reluctant to read the books she brought home, preferring to play with toys, and seemed quiet and introspective whenever school was mentioned. One day, when she was reading a bedtime story to her daughter, Lisa's mother remarked, by chance, how nice it would be when her daughter was able to read any book she wished on her own. This comment unleashed an immediate and unexpected reaction: Lisa burst into tears as all her stress and tension finally poured out. Through her tears, she explained why she had turned against school and especially against reading. Her best friend, she said, could read quietly 'in her head', and kept taunting Lisa because she was unable to do so. Even at six she had been made to feel inadequate by being upstaged by an insensitive friend.

In Lisa's case, all that was needed was reassurance. Her mother stressed how quickly Lisa was learning to read, compared with her own early struggles. The two of them planned what they would most enjoy reading together. They played schools with Lisa as teacher. Putting her in that role, while her mother read and she pointed out little mistakes, did a lot to rebuild Lisa's confidence in her own ability. Obviously, this involved Lisa's mother in a little subtle play-acting, but it helped Lisa to feel in control of her reading progress once more. Emotional problems can be caused by events which seem trivial to the adult mind; never underestimate their importance to your child. Draw on her talents. When a child is reassured and feels good about herself her work inevitably improves. A foolish word from a friend or an adult can devastate a sensitive child's confidence. Learning is often a self-fulfilling prophecy – a capable child is one who is told she is capable. A child who is expected by those around her to fail is likely not to try to succeed.

Nine times out of ten, a child who has difficulty reading will show her dissatisfaction by becoming upset when the subject is brought up in conversation. Children who don't feel sure within themselves that they can read at the same level as their friends will often try all manner of distractive strategies – from withdrawing into silence to rampaging around the room – in order to escape being faced with their own inability to master a skill they had at first assumed to be easy. As we have seen in the case of Lisa, sometimes the most simple and seemingly ludicrous worries can turn a child against reading.

Ryan's problems seemed to be more profound. Almost seven, he was disruptive in class and uncooperative in reading groups. His mother had always told him stories and rhymes, and read to him every day, but nothing she could do seemed to persuade Ryan that learning to read was worthwhile. Ryan liked to be read to but became irritable when his mother asked him to practise his reading with her. Reading practice and settling to read at all was becoming a bone of contention. Because he wouldn't sit and concentrate on learning skills that would help him to improve, his reading level was one of the lowest in his year and his teacher was both concerned at Ryan's lack of progress and stressed by his lack of attention in class.

When Ryan's mother met his teacher to discuss the problem they decided that it would be best for him to have some one-to-one help from a support teacher who worked regularly within the school. While Ryan had disliked classwork, he found studying one-to-one with a teacher trained to isolate and deal with his reading difficulties far more successful. He liked the lack of distraction and the knowledge that he had an adult concentrating on him alone. Outside the bustling classroom his impatience was not so obvious because he could ask a question and get an immediate reply. He was able to discuss exactly what kind of books he would like to read. Some were chosen especially to interest and amuse him, and he became keen enough to ask to take them home. Because his mother had always made reading a fun activity, he felt sure that she would want to share with him, so he began to read them to her and was soon telling her stories as often as she told them to him. Ryan's mother was lucky that he was at a supportive school, which had the resources to help in a swift, sensitive and practical way. She had been able to work together successfully with the school to help turn an uninterested reluctant reader into a far happier and more confident child.

Sadly, specialised one-to-one teaching is not readily available in every school. Many children in need of reading support are competing in an area of often sparse and under-funded resources; so you need to be tactfully forceful to ensure that your child gets the maximum help available. Children love reading in small groups or, even better, with just one other person so that they can be the centre of an adult's attention and admiration. Your child's school is likely to be very grateful if you can help this situation happen more often by volunteering to assist. If you are working full-time, perhaps your own partner or another family member would consider helping. Everyone in school would welcome this and schools are happy to show you how and where assistance would be most useful. Once they get used to another adult in class, shyness evaporates and children blossom in adult company. Assured of your attention, they feel free to discuss their own feelings about the books they are reading with you and this makes the whole reading experience much more enjoyable for them. It is often those readers most in need of help and experience who feel most nervous in a large group and someone who can spare the time to work with a class teacher is very valuable. Although you may not be asked to read with your own child's group, by helping to make reading an exciting time in class all the children will gain in confidence and enthusiasm.

Making reading an interesting and exciting thing to do in school is vital; once this is in place and supported by about twenty to thirty minutes of home reading every day, most children will continue to progress. If your child remains uninterested, always remember the cardinal rule – find books which please and appeal to her, and never try to impose your own views or choices without her consent. Adults often fail to talk to children on equal terms, as individuals whose ideas matter. At school, they are seldom talked to one-to-one, and it is often easy to forget how important such treatment can be for a child. Most children have their own thoughts, which they are desperately eager to convey. When your child talks to you she needs to be sure, from experience, that you will listen and be sympathetic.

A child's opportunity to communicate becomes even more vital when there is a crisis in her life. Emotional problems can preoccupy a child so much that she loses the enthusiasm for learning and her belief in her own ability to try, work and succeed. Family problems – such as separation, losing a loved one, or even something which seems superficial such as moving house – can absorb a child so thoroughly that she can find no interest in anything else. One small boy I talked to was inconsolable for a number of weeks – when I finally persuaded him to talk, he explained the reason he was so unhappy was that his house was 'all in a box'. Moving house can be a terrible trauma for young children, who have never previously experienced the turbulence it can bring, and who frequently fear that their home life will never be stable again. Be sensitive to how they feel and reassure them. There are plenty of funny books about families moving house which they will enjoy sharing with you. At school or your children's library they will be happy to recommend stories to share, which will help your child to calm down and settle back into her normal learning pattern.

If something distressing happens at home let your child know that you are always happy to talk with her. Some children feel better if they can let you know indirectly how they feel by telling or writing you a story. This can help them share with you how they really feel about a difficult or hurtful situation and enable them to express ideas which, while deeply troubling, may be only half realised. Often when something unhappy happens within their family or circle of friends they feel guilty and responsible, even though there is almost certainly no concrete reason for this. Telling a story about someone in a parallel situation releases them to say exactly what is bothering the person in their story rather than having to admit their own secret worries outright. Children who are preoccupied with any problem, no matter how minor, often fail to concentrate on other things. If they can't get their worries off their chests they can easily become even more stressed because they start to fall behind with their school work.

Throughout your child's time at school, you need to communicate comfortably and regularly with her teacher. Before you start to panic, be sure that you are looking at reading ability from the point of view of your child, and not from your own expectations. If your child is clearly unable to tackle the same level of reading as her best friend this does not necessarily mean that there is any reason or need to worry about her progress. Children are all different and all will learn to read at a different rate. As any teacher of a class of thirteen-year-olds will tell you, the children in that class are widely varying in maturity but this does not mean that they will not all eventually reach adulthood. In the same way, don't fret if your child learns to read less quickly than her friends – if a child is happy with words and continues to move on cheerfully with reading, there is little to worry about. If you find you are becoming concerned because your child does not appear to be the top achiever in class it may perhaps be you who has the problem.

If you have worked hard, and eliminated the basic practical reasons why your child might be having problems getting into reading, and you find that your child is still struggling, you may be well advised to remember the dullest truism of all – practice makes perfect. Many children who appear to be less confident readers than their classmates simply need plenty of reading practice. They need time, attention and, above all, praise – they have skills, and require only the time to consolidate them. Emphasise to a child that, just like any other skill, she cannot be expected to find reading easy immediately. Placing the facts in these terms, and comparing learning to read with other skills, such as swimming, martial arts, or tap-dancing, means that children can understand the difficulties in reading and can accept working to overcome them.

It is obviously necessary for children to know and feel comfortable with the basic skills of reading, but it is almost as important for them to care about the books they read if they are to sustain the enthusiasm to keep on. Although they were at one time out of favour, most children are engaged by reading schemes where they can follow the adventures of characters familiar from book to book. Most reading schemes are based on the repetition of very common words that need to be recognised on sight – and remember that a basic one hundred words makes up more than half of everything we read. Each book builds on any new words encountered in the book before, so children feel confident and comfortable making small steady steps forward. Children who take to reading like ducks to water can zip ahead, enjoying everything they encounter, but for the majority of children reading schemes give secure familiarity which helps them move on confidently.

Boredom can quickly make children feel disenchanted; and frustrated enough to give up on reading. Wherever possible all children should be taught in a way that they can enjoy. Learning 'key' common words can be a real trial for children who hate learning to sight-read from lists or flash cards and don't take to reading schemes. I have found one of the most successful methods of getting reluctant readers to learn to recognise words on sight is to make the words they need to learn up into bingo cards. Make these with eight or twelve words on each and make sure that you write each word used on a separate tiny card so that it can be drawn at random out of a hat or cardboard box, and then begin playing. Either involve a third person or take turns to be the caller, and ensure that every word you call is placed clearly on the table in front of your child. Make it a rule that the word picked out has to be read aloud before it can be crossed off the card. Children love this game, and when they become skilled it is easy to increase the number of words and the size of the bingo cards. Bingo is a good way of helping children to learn any phonic sounds or words that they need to know on sight but still feel wobbly about, and is a game that almost every child loves to play.

Almost equally effective is making up simple word searches. If you have access to a computer make up a small grid. List the words you are helping your child to learn below the grid and hide them within it among random letters. Concentrating on reading each word from the list and searching intensely for it fascinates children and gives them a thrill when they succeed, as well as teaching them far more than they realise. There are ready-made grids and lists of words for you to photocopy, cut up and use at the end of the book which can save you time.

A lot of tried and tested card games can be adapted to make learning to read words or phonics more fun. Snap is jolly and effective. Copy about twenty words or phonemes clearly on to postcards – one on each card – duplicate the set and play. Five sets of snap cards can provide an easy way of teaching and practising all one hundred of the most basic common keywords and give your child a lot of fun in the process – but make sure that everyone has to say the word before they cry 'snap!'.

You can use these same sets of word or sound postcards to make a pairs memory game. Shuffle them, and lay them face down on a flat surface. Then ask each person playing to turn over two cards to try and pair them up. As well as teaching reading, this game helps children to learn observation, concentration and remembering, and is a lot of fun for everyone playing.

Children are brilliant at making up their own games. Once you have sets of word or sound postcards, ask them to devise a good game to play or help them to make up a board game where every square they could land on has a phoneme, word or message written on it. More confident readers can make games with forfeit cards or messages on every square. These are fun to make and play with, and practise both reading and working things out systematically.

Most reading schemes are excellent for teaching children to master the most common words in written English on sight. So if your child is unhappy with her school reading scheme, it is well worth seeking out a more enjoyable one. If you want to choose a relaxed gradual reading scheme for your child, look for one that starts simply and moves on steadily, repeating and building on words that have been learned already. Many children find revision lists of words at the back of every book a comfort and their confidence is continually boosted when they manage to read through them successfully alone. Reading one scheme at home, and another at school, is unlikely to confuse your child – remember, as long as she enjoys reading, any books are a success.

Don't be afraid to use 'old-fashioned' reading schemes: they have stood the test of time and could be equally well loved by children today as they were by another generation. Dr

Seuss, and the 'Janet and John' books, are still lovely introductions to reading, practising basic words, sounds and rhymes bound up in memorable story-telling and humour. Children don't find stories written about the world as it was in their parents' and grandparents' younger lives particularly strange. In fact, their slightly outdated peculiarities seem to give them a sort of fairy-tale magic. If you have loved a book or a comic when you started reading, find a copy and read it with your child. They will pick up your enthusiasm and want to share it with you. Sugar the pill by using laughter and games. All you need is a pen, felt-tip colours, some postcards or paper and a little imagination.

Children who like playing schools will most probably enjoy filling in worksheets. Just write or type a simple sentence on a sheet of paper with one or two basic words left out – you can always put a little picture in each space as a clue. If the child you are working with gets stuck, try some other words to see if they make sense in the sentence – stupidly inappropriate words that will make her laugh are best – before you suggest the 'right' one and help her to write it down. Words are far easier to learn in context than in isolation and most 'key' words are difficult to illustrate visually, so need to be anchored either through a game or as part of a memorable sentence or story.

Alice had been bringing home basic words to learn for over a year, but she never seemed to read or bother with them. Her school didn't use a reading scheme that brought them repeatedly into the text and Alice was having trouble because to her every book seemed to be full of brand-new words and she could hardly recognise any on sight. Alice's family got her involved by helping her to turn her learning into a game that she would be very much in charge of. They helped Alice to buy a blank exercise book where they labelled one half of the first-page spread 'Alice will' and the opposite side 'Alice won't'. Just by playing and talking together, they soon had two long lists of things that Alice was prepared to do (get presents) and not prepared to do (eat slugs). This was very easy to build on with contrasts on every page spread. One page for things that go up, one for things that go down, one for in and one for out; there were almost endless possibilities. Alice had her own thoughts for every one, loved making the book, and remembered and understood almost every word she used. There are some ideas for books to make with your child to help her learn at the back of this book.

With practice, Alice became more certain of her ability to read and to write what she wanted. She turned some of her list ideas into stories for her younger brother, first with her mother and later by herself. Alice's family had capitalised on her love of expressing her own opinions and her delight in being heard to help her to learn by helping herself and having fun.

Surprisingly to many adults, children often enjoy spelling words out loud, particularly if they are sure that they have got them right. A great incentive to a young child playing this game is to allow her to cheat a little – place a list of the words you want her to read and spell out just close enough for her to sneak a glance at it if she gets stuck and then ask her to spell one of them. Every time she gets one right, pop a marble into a jar in front of her and see how long it takes to fill the jar up – a full jar could be the passport to a treat. As they get more confident and familiar with the same words coming up in the game over and over again, children steal fewer and fewer glimpses to check up on themselves. They don't panic because they know that they have the means to get every word right if they really need it.

Lee didn't like working with other people. He would

always try to opt out of group games, preferring to sit alone with his own work. Although he would sit quietly in class, he hated having to read or spell anything out loud in front of other people. His basic shyness was made worse because, although he was good at building up words phonetically, irregularly spelt words, particularly those that looked alike, puzzled and disturbed him because he couldn't work them out successfully. Lee had real difficulty determining the difference between superficially similar words, such as 'though' and 'through'. One day when she was listening to him read, his teacher realised what was happening and worked out ways to help that would suit Lee's reticent personality. Because he obviously felt most comfortable sitting by himself and getting on with things, she decided to make him his own worksheets. First they read them through together so that they could work out the best answers. Then Lee settled down on his own to fill them in. In the first worksheet his teacher asked him to colour in the word 'through' in yellow every time he read it and to colour 'though' green. Lee studied the sheet intently and, remembering what he had been told, took obvious enjoyment in meticulously and quite correctly filling it in. This very simple strategy made it possible to teach Lee to recognise the difference between words he had previously found confusing. Just by showing him clearly what each word meant and which was which, letting him read a simple story and have some quiet fun colouring in, his reading became more assured.

Recognising children's need for privacy and making their reading work into an enjoyable game that can, with guidance, be played alone, can prove very successful when working with the more reticent among them. But you do need to gently run through the work with them first and repeat anything that they don't seem to fully understand. They will become even less sure of themselves if they are given work without thoroughly understanding how to undertake it. Any word game must necessarily be enjoyable for the children taking part if they are to learn from it successfully. If you find that they have got things wrong, correct their mistakes quickly and gently in a matter-of-fact way, but never be over-critical, and always stress their progress and praise all the things that they have done right. Quiet, self-effacing children are often easily embarrassed by their mistakes, and having them pointed out in a censorious way may hurt them and stop them wanting to try again.

Children who like playing schools are often happy to 'repeat' lessons at home, especially if the roles are reversed and they are in charge and teaching you, because they build up confidence by feeling in control. Big books are really useful for this and are beginning to be available in most bookshops (see lists at the back of this book). Help by holding the book up where you can both see it and remember to read the words your child is pointing to when she tells you to do it. Children make notoriously strict teachers.

Even though many basic words are hard to illustrate, others can be made more memorable if they are linked with an appropriate picture. Remembering the word 'apple' next to a picture of a big rosy apple is one of the first memories of learning to read for most English-speaking people. Even verbs are relatively easy to explain – simply write down the word you wish your child to learn and draw the appropriate action. Jumping, hopping, reading, running – it is easy to draw or find pictures of children doing things. Try making scrap-books together by cutting pictures out of comics and magazines, or off food packaging, and labelling the actions. Or find a picture of a street or playground and label what everyone is doing in it.

If you are working with more than one child, try making

a group of cards with verbs (very obvious 'activity words') written upon them. Ask your children to pick up and read the card (with help if they need it) and then act out the action linked to that word. You will soon find yourself in the middle of a game in which every child is desperate to be the first to have a go. While it is possible to play this game one-to-one, it is usually more fun, and often more successful, with a small, competitive crowd. This game is so popular with some of the children I have worked with that they now demand it at parties.

More abstract words can't be learned so easily in this way. Again, making lists works well for many children. Setting down their hates and loves, likes and dislikes, and things that make them happy and unhappy keeps them focused and learning, and the information can also be stuck up on their walls as a grisly warning for any potential baby-sitters. Children love the concrete power that writing lists can give, ordering how they feel about things in a way that other people can read and take notice of. Another way of showing any child how useful words can be is by leaving notes for her around the house or simple instructions like 'Please close this door'. Use every opportunity to practise reading, by giving her words that are fun, or have a useful function.

By their second year of school, most children like to feel secure that they are making considerable progress with their reading. However, if you think anxiety is affecting your child's learning it is obviously important not to tell her off but to observe her sensitively and talk with her to find out what is wrong. Common sense will tell you that getting irritable with her will make her even more anxious to the point where she will be too scared to read at all. Children are almost always more acutely aware of their weak spots than their strengths, and more in need of praise than criticism. Mastering the skills of reading requires understanding the expertise involved, coupled with security and a belief that they can and they will eventually succeed in whatever they want or need to do.

Don't put on any more pressure. If your child brings a reading book home but seems to be reluctant to read to you, ask if you can share her reading with her. Curiosity will normally mean a child is eager to learn what the book she has brought home tells her, even if she has difficulty deciphering it herself. Always read to your child and with her even if she is reluctant to read to you. Try to tempt her into reading along with you, by asking her to predict the plot of the story, or to compare characters with her own experiences. But don't worry if she doesn't take the hint. Far better for your child that you continue to read enjoyably with her, than that you create the impression you are worried, and worry her in turn. Don't make children read if they don't want to, but encourage them and reward them with praise, or even a small treat if they do. Read *with* your child, rather than *to* her. You will soon find you are enjoying yourself, talking with your child about the stories you read together.

Once again, it is important to remember to use whatever reading material catches your child's attention. Catalogues fascinate children, so read through them together. Children will try really hard to decipher information about toys written in a catalogue although they might otherwise show very little interest in reading at all. Even looking through the clothes and household sections with them is worthwhile because they enjoy being able to link the written descriptions with the accompanying pictures. This is a great way of talking about how best to describe something – what size and shape is it? What colour? What does it feel like? What is it used for? All this helps a child to think and order what she wants to say as well as building up her store of words.

Often pets inflame fierce loyalties. Find books about how best to keep them and make up a 'Pet Book' of photos and stories about them. Try taking a blank book on holiday with you, and writing and drawing something about what happens each day. Ask grandparents to write a simple story about their own lives or just write down things that you remember from childhood that you think your child might like to read about. One boy I worked with showed no interest whatsoever in reading until his parents bought a different car. He spent weeks filling a book with photos and drawings of it and even tried to read the handbook. Anything that provides the spark to get a child reading is very valuable, no matter how bizarre it may seem.

When you do talk with them you will realise that children have their own stories, which are simply waiting to be written down. Listen to them, offer to write down what they say and help them make their own books – there are few greater encouragements than seeing your own words in print! If you have a computer, use it. That way, you can produce a book similar to those your child expects to see at school or at home. But if you don't have a computer, just writing down your child's stories will make them a source of great pride for both of you, now and in the future, and will mean they can be read again and again. At first, you may be reading her stories to her – later, she will be reading her stories to you.

When your child does want to begin reading with any book or comic, encourage her interest by talking about the pictures and explaining how they relate to the text. Any difficulties with particular words can easily be solved if you read it for her quickly and explain what it means in that context. Encourage her to use phonics to work out words she is not sure of by taking them apart and building them up again, but don't force things if she seems to be getting fretful – it is more effective to tell a child the word that she is finding difficult to read rather than push her hard if she is having real trouble deciphering it phonetically. It helps most children if you can point at each word to be read as they go along and if your child doesn't work out a particular word within a few seconds, don't make an issue of it – reveal the word and keep the momentum going.

Although you understand your own child best, it is also true that her teacher is the only person who sees her frequently in class conditions. Try hard to consider her teacher's opinions because, generally, they are intended to benefit your child. There are regular school checks on every child's reading, and you will obviously make more progress at home if you can talk things over with her teachers and fully understand any difficulties your child is having at school. This works both ways and your child's teacher has much to learn from you. If you notice particular difficulties continually coming up when you are listening to your child read do tell her teacher. The teacher is almost certainly doing his or her best to be alert to individual cases but it is often hard to spot problems in a quiet pupil when there is a full noisy class vying for attention.

One useful way of relaying news about your child's reading, what books she likes or dislikes and whether her reading levels seem comfortably suitable, is by parents and teachers communicating through a child's individual home/school book. As the name suggests, this is a shared diary in which a child's progress is noted in turn by her teacher, and her parent. Try to bear in mind that any criticism given by a teacher is intended to help your child – the teacher wants to encourage reading as much as you do. When a parent is anxious (as all parents are) about a child's progress with reading at school it is easy to be extra sensitive about any comments that are made. Be careful not to take comments about your child's reading at home as implied criticism – home/school books are intended to help your child through encouraging communication between home and school. If any written comments are in some way making you feel hurt and resentful, try to talk to your child's teacher face to face to prevent misunderstandings. Sometimes parents and teachers do disagree about how best to teach a particular child to read and what books are most suitable for her, and it is important to talk this out and reach a compromise without affecting the child involved.

When you are sharing books with a child and trying to help her get more experience of reading, it is easy to become obsessed with words and forget just how radically their meaning can be altered by punctuation. As you read with your child, be sure to point out punctuation marks and explain what they do as you come to them. It's easy to show by the volume and tone of your voice the effect that an exclamation or question mark has in a sentence. Practise the difference in how best to say 'Please will you help me!' and 'Please will you help me?' together. Full stops and commas can be worked out in much the same way by pausing and taking a long or short breath in the appropriate places. When you are reading to a child always be guided by the direction that punctuation gives you and when she is reading to you show her how to use it to help her get over the exact meaning of every word.

Most families help their children to practise reading in less than ideal circumstances. What they had intended to be a meaningful, relaxed, bonding experience gets turned into a frantic breakfast-time row, or a hurried moment last thing at night. The only way out of this is to find a way to make time. Bedtime is ideal. This will also mean that they are reading at a time when they expect to do nothing else. Television, video and computer games are formidable competition, and it is almost impossible to turn a child from a game or favourite television programme to reading practice without a battle. By reading with your child in bed, you will create in her mind a feeling that she is getting a treat and being allowed to stay awake longer than normal, something which she is sure to regard as a good thing.

But even when everyone involved is trying their hardest to help, not all early difficulties with reading are simply and easily resolved. For a child with a mental or a physical disability, particularly one which is not noticed immediately, learning to read can be a difficult, uphill struggle. As we shall see in the next chapter, physical and mental problems with reading can be helped by thorough, efficient and sympathetic assessment, attention and expert help. Not all difficulties can be solved but they can be made a lot less stressful and debilitating.

3

Specific Learning Difficulties – Fact and Fiction

All children have individual strengths and weaknesses. Some will flourish under a highly structured reading programme while others prefer a broader, more relaxed approach. Obviously, to learn to read effectively all children will need organisation, confidence in their abilities, and a great deal of patience both from within themselves and from their teachers in a school and a home setting. As fundamental as any of these is the desire to read. Instilling a love of language from an early age, and an understanding of the liberation that reading can bring, is a great step towards making your child a happy and successful reader.

Love of reading begins long before reading itself is taught. By telling your child stories and rhymes from an early age, you will help to instil a love of speech and language long before he is immersed in the formal learning process. The most enthusiastic readers often associate reading with happiness and security because this had always been the case when they were young children sharing books with their family at home. Learning basic words by sight and understanding, remembering and using phonics, are necessary processes, enabling children to read more quickly and effectively; but it is not the structure of words that forms the most important aspect either of reading or the desire to read. A child will want to bother to learn to read because of the magic he has been taught words can obtain. The power to reveal stories and teach facts is the only one which can keep a child continually interested in the reading process.

Although it is difficult to pin-point a precise age when your child should be reading successfully, most children of seven can read a book alone. If your child finds reading difficult at this age, don't worry him by overstressing his difficulties because this will simply lead to panic and cause your child to regard reading not as a source of pleasure, but of distress. Never compare a child unfavourably with others; always remain positive, and stress that difficulties are not an impermeable barrier but minor problems that can be worked through with time and tolerance.

When a child begins to read within the formal surroundings of a school, he is given a great deal of work from the start. On average, he will be expected to learn one or two words on sight each day, and master at least one phonic skill, the capacity to distinguish one phoneme from another, a week. A class of children will, inevitably, have to be taught a consistent method because no normal school has the time or high enough staffing levels to teach all children individually. But, just as inevitable is the fact that each child will learn most effectively in the manner which suits his individual capabilities and interests.

The use of phonics as a teaching technique clearly illustrates the sort of discrepancies which occur from child to child. While some children find it easy to read with little reference to the phonic system, learning simply by use of the look-and-say method of immediate sight-reading, others find it extremely difficult to decipher words without reference to their phonic building blocks. Understanding how written letters (graphemes) correspond to sounds (phonemes) underpins the process of reading. As well as the alphabetical phonemes, a good comprehension of words relies on a firm knowledge of phonic clusters – the blends or groups of letters at the beginning, middle or end of words. Even a seemingly simple letter cluster, such as 'str', needs to be recognised as three letter sounds – s, t, and r – pronounced so closely together that they form one single unit. In total there are over forty phonemes which your child must master, some made distinct from one another only by the most subtle of sound differences.

A further difficulty to the learning of phonemes is the fact that, in English in particular, certain phonic sounds are reliant upon variant spellings. 'ai', 'eigh', and 'ay' all form the same phoneme and sound the same, yet are separate and distinct graphemes which look very different from one another written down. Even though the relationship between sounds and letters is not always straightforward, a child who holds a broad knowledge of phonics possesses an efficient way of deciphering words which might otherwise remain a mystery. A crowded school class must necessarily be taught a combination of methods which are tolerable and effective for most, yet ideal for few. When you hear your child read, you need to listen very sensitively to try to pick up any pattern of mistakes.

We have already seen how even a very slight hearing deficiency can alter the way in which a child perceives individual phonic sounds. Each unit of sound (phoneme) is represented by certain letters or letter groups (graphemes) so the way a child hears and learns a grapheme can radically affect how he reads a word. If deficiencies such as this go undetected in the early stages of learning they can lead to deep-seated reading difficulties.

Most people with a reading difficulty would have been fine if it had been diagnosed and they had been given appropriate help at an early age. While a six-year-old child will often enjoy increased individual attention, an eight-year-old can come to regard any outside help as an embarrassment he would rather avoid. As they get older, children are more and more keen to conform and they often hate to be picked for 'extra' teaching – feeling that they have been singled out as failures. Children who haven't been given the means to learn and are not able to get the help they need, feel isolated and many take refuge in behaving badly. Often, being regarded as the class trouble-maker helps them to feel that they have a status and releases them from needing to be anything else. Many children who have been permanently or temporarily excluded from school have endured reading difficulties for much of their academic life. These children are often disruptive and totally uninvolved with lessons because they cannot decipher the work they are given. Some feel even more alienated and insulted because they are set obviously different and 'easier' work to do. This can be very dispiriting, since many poor readers are capable of excellent reasoning and can tackle complex ideas. Many behave as if they feel that teachers are deliberately searching for devious ways of giving them work at which they will fail in a humiliating and very public way. Children who can't read capably often opt out of learning simply because they aren't given the means to learn. They shout at teachers to get in first and in those circumstances it is supremely difficult for a teacher to help them with an understanding heart.

But there are of course cases when attention and care are not enough – when a child has a genuine physical or mental difficulty with learning to read. Probably the most common physical problem affecting a child's ability to read is poor hearing. Even those with only minor hearing difficulties, which can often be complex to diagnose, may find reading extremely hard. Such children can have great trouble learning to read phonetically, as they literally cannot distinguish between certain extremely similar phonemes like b and p.

A common hearing difficulty, and one which is often undetected at a pre-school age, is an inability to hear particular frequencies of sound. The normal human speech range varies between one hundred and four thousand cycle frequencies per second. If a child has a hearing loss in any part of this range, he will be forced to guess at part of what is spoken. Different hearing difficulties will affect a child in different ways – a hearing loss in the high-frequency range of the human voice will, for example, make it particularly hard to distinguish consonant sounds. A child with a hearing loss in this range will have problems perceiving the difference between similar consonants, such as s, z, ch and sh. It is extremely difficult, in a classroom of more than thirty children, for any teacher to identify these subtle hearing weaknesses. Children assume that the sound they hear is the correct sound: the normal one that everyone else hears. If, unknown to them, they are in fact mishearing sounds they become unsure, frustrated and sometimes even frightened because they just don't understand where they are going wrong.

One reason that minor hearing difficulties go initially undetected is that, in the context of a home, familiarity makes it particularly easy for a child to understand a parent's speech pattern, regardless of any minor hearing difficulties he has. For example, Polly spent her first four years at home with her mother, and later her baby brother. Hers was a very self-contained family; however, Polly's mother had noticed that when her own parents visited, Polly did not always understand what they said. A further warning sign, which she gradually noticed, was that Polly's early exuberance and friendliness at school soon cooled, and she was becoming quieter and more withdrawn. Alerted by these slight danger signs, she arranged to have her daughter's hearing checked and discovered that she had problems which, despite prior examinations, were undiagnosed. Both Polly and her mother had become so used to each other that, although Polly sometimes did not hear words clearly, she found it easy to predict or decipher what her mother had meant to say. In the less ordered class atmosphere, Polly had extreme difficulty perceiving what was being said. Quite naturally, assuming that her hearing was normal and that she was hearing the same words as everyone else in the class, she could not comprehend why she kept getting instructions wrong and couldn't understand what was going on around her.

At times, it is easier for an outsider to notice a child's slight hearing difficulties than for a parent, who lives with his personal idiosyncrasies every day. If you suspect your child may have such problems, there are certain signs which can help to confirm your suspicions. A child will always repeat what he hears; in the case of one with minor deafness, this may not be what is spoken. If your child has unclear speech – particularly at the ends of words – this may be a sign that he is having difficulty hearing and distinguishing phonemes accurately.

Andrew was a happy and contented child at home but, to the amazement of his family, during his third term at school he rapidly became so aggressive and disruptive that he was excluded three times. During his first term, Andrew had got along well with other children and, despite flashes of ill temper on his part, had a good relationship with his class teacher. His usual teacher, Mrs A, had been teaching for many years and had come to know most of the reading books she used with the class from memory. This meant that very often when she taught reading, using either a blackboard or a large-print book, she was sufficiently confident to remain turned towards the children while reading the words beside her. She had noticed over the course of his first two terms at school that Andrew tended to study her very carefully when she read and had assumed that this was simply because he was a particularly attentive child.

In Andrew's third term the class was frequently taught by Miss B, a final-year student. Although rapidly becoming a very competent teacher, Miss B was relatively inexperienced and she only felt comfortable when everyone, including herself, had their faces turned towards the book they were learning from. When she was reading to the class from a big book, something that happened every day, she had to crane her head round to read it as she held it up for the children to see and Andrew had no chance of seeing her lips move. Unknown to anyone in school or at home, Andrew had been deciphering the sounds of words said and read to him mainly through lip-reading. With the advent of Miss B he had been left, suddenly, with few means of understanding the words which were read, as he had real difficulty distinguishing between certain sounds. At home, his family had unconsciously grown used to making allowances for his hearing difficulties and watching him as they spoke. Now that he was unable to follow stories by lip-reading his teacher he felt left out, frustrated and angry. As a student teacher, Miss B had trouble dealing with the rages which followed and Andrew became so violently disruptive that he sometimes had to be excluded.

It was after Andrew was excluded from school that a teacher, working with him one-to-one, came to realise he only seemed to fully understand what she said to him when he was watching her lips carefully. When he had a teacher to himself, who could concentrate on his needs alone, Andrew could lip-read and comprehend everything that was going on and he began to relax. When he was tested, it became clear that Andrew had previously undetected hearing difficulties. It was when his strategies for coping with deafness were confronted with new and difficult barriers that his behavioural problems began. With his hearing difficulties corrected, Andrew eventually settled happily back into school and learning once more.

Not all children with hearing problems are as difficult as Andrew and this can make their problems even harder to detect. Some teachers have remarked to me that children with hearing difficulties can often seem extremely good-natured. Afraid of the reaction which his problems might cause, a child will frequently smile and pretend he understands If you are worried about your child's hearing in any way, it is essential that you ask your doctor to arrange a detailed examination and assessment. Be sure to tell your child's teacher immediately and he or she will keep a special eye out for problems, and may well also introduce you to the teacher responsible for children with special educational needs within that school. This teacher will probably be referred to as the SENCO (Special Educational Needs Co-ordinator) and will take a special interest in the findings of your child's hearing assessment, as well as helping to ensure that any recommendations the hearing specialists make for the education of your child within the school are carried out.

Obviously, clear, efficient eyesight, and an ability to track print accurately, are essential for everyone learning to read by sight. Children have both hearing and sight tests throughout childhood but still some slip through the net and it is often more complex than one might at first suspect to detect visual difficulties. A normal eye, faced with a written passage which the reader finds difficult, will track each line erratically and haphazardly. It is the unexpected complexity of the passage and the consequent problems reading it that causes the erratic movement, rather than poor eyesight.

Every child needs to be taught to read print in rows and to track and scan each line of text, until with time the motion becomes almost unconscious. A small number of children have difficulties in keeping both eyes consistently in focus. This means that the print they see is blurred and unclear. If you see your child moving his head from right to left as he reads, rather than his eyes, or if he prefers to read with one eye covered, this could indicate that he has trouble focusing both eyes on the text. Headaches and complaints about trouble with balance can also be warning signs. A few children have an over-sensitivity to the glare of white paper; this can cause blurred or 'moving' print, which leads to headaches that make deciphering print a miserable process. In some cases it is possible for this problem to be solved in a relatively simple way by using a coloured plastic overlay, or tinted glasses.

Some children are happy, well taught, physically and mentally totally fit and well, but still find reading an almost impenetrable problem. Developmental dyslexia is defined by Macdonald Critchley in *The Dyslexic Child* as 'a disorder of children who, despite conventional classroom experience, fail to attain the language skills of reading, writing and spelling, commensurate with their intellectual abilities'. This covers a wide range of problems, so the professionals talk of different 'dyslexias', not of a single category. Few people who have worked with young readers will deny that dyslexias do exist and can make problems that cause those affected great distress. But sometimes a child arrives 'labelled' by parents or a previous teacher as dyslexic when in fact his difficulties stem from poor teaching or previously undiagnosed disabilities.

The term dyslexia can, however, be controversial. It makes

some psychologists and educationalists very hot under the collar, as they argue against its very existence. In the dyslexia debate, both sides are convinced they are absolutely correct, and both sides frequently assume extreme positions. The British Dyslexia Association argues that four per cent of the population suffer from a form of dyslexia; one brochure, indeed, places the number closer to ten per cent. The Association feels that more care should be taken to increase awareness that dyslexia is a 'disorder of higher cerebral function' hindering an affected child from developing the basic mechanism for specific skills. The result of this disorder is that children of average, or above-average intelligence in most areas can have very poor skills in reading, writing, or mathematics. According to believers in the physical cause of dyslexia, certain signs can indicate that a child suffers from the disorder from a very early age. These include delays in speech development coupled with a persistent tendency to confuse words, constant difficulty with everyday tasks such as tying shoelaces and fastening buttons, clumsiness, poor co-ordination and a limited concentration span. Difficulty repeating polysyllabic words (words like necessary and fascinating that are made up of several syllables) can also serve as an indication. A nonsense polysyllabic word like nonfuntabulist will prove particularly difficult for dyslexic children to make out as they tend to have serious trouble segmenting phonemes and syllables.

Some dyslexic children of primary school age are missed by early screening tests. This is because they have managed to achieve a reading age above the cut-off point of the tester; however, they are still not reading to the level their natural ability would suggest. Subtle indicators of early dyslexias are a reversal of numbers and letters, difficulty telling left from right, real problems learning sequences such as months and multiplication tables, and continued trouble with buttons, shoelaces, skipping, ball games and concentration.

A child with indications of dyslexia will often work slowly in class, and may find copying from a blackboard or taking notes a tortuous task. Some dyslexic children find language a puzzle, and cannot even decipher a meaning from certain texts when they have been read correctly. Some will find spelling a fundamental difficulty; others may perform well in spelling tests, but revert to bizarre word constructions in their own free writing. Although dyslexias can go unnoticed at first, parents often sense that there is something 'wrong'. Their child may seem frustrated and unhappy, particularly when trying hard to learn, and it is important to watch for these warning signs. They don't of themselves definitely mean that an individual child has this specific learning problem but it is obviously better to assess possible dyslexias swiftly and thoroughly rather than to wait for any 'symptoms' to go away.

Richard was finally excluded from school following a repeated refusal to attend, which had lasted for over six months. He was an alert, sensitive boy who had always found school work that demanded reading and writing frustrating. Although he could answer questions in lessons where everything was clearly explained, his written work was invariably so misspelt that he was often teased. On the surface Richard seemed to be taking the jibes in good part but at heart he was so deeply upset that his school absences grew longer. At first the stress was making him feel genuinely sick and his non-attendance could be put down to poor health. But gradually days away from school developed into weeks and months and it was obvious that Richard was refusing to go to school again, rather than being physically ill.

Richard was lucky, his parents and his school worked

together to get him help and support. He went into school for a limited time every week where he worked one-to-one with a teacher who devised an individual programme appropriate to his needs. By using a structured system of text organisation, and learning to understand the phonic building blocks of words, Richard's spelling and his reading confidence started to improve. Concentrating on learning basic words and phonics, he also worked out mnemonics to help him spell and remember lists of facts that he needed to learn. But as soon as he began free writing, rather than concentrating on individual words, his spelling and to some extent his sentence construction started to disintegrate. Over time, his reading improved so much that he could read what he wanted at last but it was clearly apparent that Richard had a specific problem with spelling when he tried to write for himself. He was assessed by an educational psychologist who confirmed that he had a specific learning difficulty. Dyslexias are usually referred to as specific learning difficulties (SpLD) and Richard felt more confident in his own ability to overcome his problem once he knew that it had been acknowledged.

Children inevitably tease each other but most are sympathetic to another's disability once they realise it exists and understand the perplexity it brings about. Slowly Richard's confidence grew and he gradually spent longer and longer in school until, boosted by new friendships and extra teaching support, he was finally totally re-integrated. Everyone he dealt with in school understood his problems and almost all were keen to help him. Working on a computer, where he could constantly spell-check words he was unsure of proved a breakthrough for him. At last he had the chance to produce work to the standards he had wanted to achieve all along.

If you feel that your child shows indications of suffering a specific learning difficulty, the most successful way to communicate with his school is to talk with his SENC. The school, coupled with support services, will then work out how best to investigate your child's problem thoroughly. They will work to determine whether your child suffers from chronic learning difficulties, or a simpler problem with learning that normal school remedial resources could solve. If they feel the trouble is chronic, your child's school may ask the Local Education Authority (LEA) to arrange for a statutory assessment of his educational needs. This will be a very detailed examination designed to discover exactly what your child's particular educational needs are and all the special help that he or she may require. This will be set out clearly in a 'statement' detailing his specific learning problems together with the provision that should be made to help him. This statement may ensure that your child gets definite access to certain types of additional assistance. The LEA will make a statement when they decide after appropriate thorough assessment that all the extra help your child needs can't reasonably be provided within the resources normally available to the school. These include money, staff time and special equipment, so if your child does have a statement, additional resources could be found to help him.

Parents as well as schools can ask their LEA to provide a statutory assessment with a view, hopefully, to getting a statement of their child's special educational needs. This can seem very daunting but the whole process is explained more fully in chapter six.

If your child is diagnosed, by an educational psychologist, as possessed of a specific learning disorder, he will be offered help within the school which will conform fairly accurately to his own individual needs. Whenever possible, your child's teacher should make the time to discuss the content of the lesson with him and explain any major points. Your child may also be offered support in class during some of his lessons. Often this help will come from a non-teaching assistant, who will both explain the lesson orally, and act as an interpreter whenever he encounters print which causes him difficulty. Sometimes, children may also be helped to tape-record lessons so that they can reinforce what they have learned in the lesson by repeating it at home. Most children with an acknowledged specific learning difficulty will spend some time learning one-to-one with a learning support teacher. Sometimes time is cleared for this by dropping subjects like modern languages which place extra strain on a child who finds working with words painfully hard. As with overcoming all problems, the common sense of perseverance, organisation and the belief in his own ability to win through is vitally important. But children suffering from specific learning difficulties can't just psych themselves up to buckle down and get on with it because they have very real problems with organisation and remembering. They need teachers and helpers who can transmit confidence by being patient, positive and persevering in their teaching methods. They need to teach children to listen to, recognise and understand every individual letter and sound that makes up a word and effectively to teach all the simple and complicated phonic rules, both for individual and blended letter sounds (phonemes) in words, which are the tools they will need to enable them to sound out regular words. They also need to teach children to link irregularly spelt words directly with their meaning to make them more memorable.

Children handicapped by dyslexias learn to read and spell most effectively if they are taught with a structured system that relies on hearing and touch as much as visual recognition. Their low self-esteem can cause many 'dyslexic' children to seem inattentive, slow or badly behaved, qualities that can make teachers hostile rather than sympathetic. To be effective, any remedial teaching relies on a thorough in-depth assessment and understanding of a child's problems. Sadly, the term 'dyslexic' can often just become a blanket 'diagnosis' that covers all children with a reading disorder and suggests that they all suffer from the same problems; and the crucial differences in every individual child are all too easily ignored. To help in the most positive way possible, teachers need an exact picture of reading, spelling, or other difficulties that the child they are working with is labouring under to enable them to make the best use of the time they have together. Children who give indications that they have reading and spelling problems need to be given far more rigorous and accurate testing to enable their individual needs to be identified and worked with.

Early intervention and in-depth assessment is common sense because if help is only offered later in a child's school it is likely to be far more expensive in terms of resources and it will take longer to be effective. If a child starts school handicapped by a language or learning difficulty, especially one which limits his ability to distinguish phonemes, understanding reading and spelling is likely to be a confusing, frustrating ordeal. He will start to expect to fail, and his belief in his own ability to learn could be torn to shreds. This should never be allowed to happen – disruptive children are far more likely to be handicapped by a learning difficulty than motivated by naughtiness. They need effective assessment and help early to prevent any possibility that they slip through the net.

Many disaffected, disruptive children and teenagers miss out on their education (and distract others around them from learning) because their needs have never been fully assessed and taken care of. This is particularly true of children who have specific learning difficulties because they can often appear simply not to be trying. They are verbally bright but just don't seem to be paying attention or taking enough care with the presentation of their work whereas, if the truth were known, they are mortified and desperately upset by their inability to set down their own thoughts in a way that would elicit much sought-after praise from their teachers.

Some children who show every sign that they are affected by dyslexias suffer from problems stemming from colour blindness. The Corneal Laser Centre at the Clatterbridge Hospital in Cheshire have worked with people who have had problems reading words all their lives. By providing small groups of people previously diagnosed as dyslexic with colour-filtered Chroma-Gen lenses, the Centre has enabled them to successfully read text which had previously appeared jumbled and confused. Some of the people taking part in the trials were so severely colour-blind that they saw the world in shades of grey but the specially selected Chroma-Gen lenses helped them to distinguish colour and form at last.

Each lens contains a minute colour filter which prevents light from certain key frequencies entering the eye. For some of the people taking part in the tests this has given them the ability to see print clearly and comfortably so that they can learn to read effectively at last. At the time of writing only small-scale studies have been carried out with Chroma-Gen lenses. Although results are very encouraging, far more extensive trials will need to take place before their effectiveness can be confirmed.

A further argument serving to undermine the simple belief that all dyslexia is caused by neurological disorder stems from evidence supplied by psychologist Michael Rutter, and his team of researchers, in the 1970s. They found that the number of children suffering from the reading difficulties which might be termed dyslexia was four times greater in those from

London than in those from the Isle of Wight. In the course
of their research, Rutter and his team firmly identified a group
of children whose tested intelligence was high, but who suffered from abnormally low literacy – but far from concluding
that they had determined decisive proof concerning the existence of dyslexia, Michael Rutter and his team found that a
child's environment, teaching, family input, stability at school
and temperament were of far greater significance to his ultimate reading level than biological factors. As Rutter power-
fully concludes,

> In short, there has been a complete failure to show that
> the signs of dyslexia constitute any meaningful pattern. It
> may be concluded that the question of whether specific
> reading retardation is or is not dyslexia can be abandoned
> as meaningless.

But there may be more going on here than at first meets the
eye. Dr Beve Hornsby cites Michael Rutter's study in her
book *Overcoming Dyslexia*, commenting that the discrepancy between levels of reading difficulty encountered between
the groups studied in London and the Isle of Wight, was in
part caused by social conditions:

> In poor urban communities there are often a number of
> factors that make learning difficult: immigrant families'
> lack of knowledge of the English language, large families
> inadequately housed, poor diet, environmental pollution,
> lack of sleep, poor health and a possible lack of interest
> in books and literacy. Add to this the fact that the average
> number of books in the home is 1.2 and that many people
> do not consider literacy important and so do not, or per-
> haps cannot, read to their children, it is not surprising that

the percentage of dyslexic children in less well off sectors of society is so high.

But, in direct contrast with Rutter's reasoning, Hornsby also concludes that while reading difficulties are aggravated by environment and lack of learning opportunities there remains nevertheless a specific neurological disorder which must be termed 'dyslexia'. If you feel that your child may be handicapped by any of the specific learning difficulties that come under the umbrella heading of 'dyslexia' you need to find the means to have his problems expertly assessed as soon as possible.

The debate about the specifics of dyslexia continues, but in the context of your child it is important not to assume that simply because he has difficulties reading he is 'dyslexic'. As we have already seen, many normal, intelligent children suffer reading problems because of poor teaching, visual, hearing or emotional problems. While dyslexia might seem like a blessed explanation of your child's difficulties, it is not always a correct or constructive one.

Jan developed reading difficulties following an accident which caused several severe breaks to her left arm during the summer term of her second year in school. She finally recovered well but seemed to be finding her school work increasingly hard and, although an intelligent and imaginative child, was experiencing a lot of trouble reading and writing. Concerned, her mother began to fear that Jan might be dyslexic and almost in panic watched her every move, looking for clues that might back up this 'diagnosis'. In fact, Jan's problems were brought about by her long absence from school. During all her time away Jan had lost touch with how the rest of the class had been progressing. She had missed out on the phonics and words that they had learned together as well as on the books they had enjoyed as a class. Illness and being away from school for a long time are inevitably isolating experiences and when she returned Jan felt overwhelmed by all the things that school friends had learned. The gaps in her learning made her feel left out and she was too depressed and unmotivated to ask about things she didn't know. By helping her with games devised to make learning more accessible, her teacher, family and friends slowly reassured Jan and helped her to make up everything she had missed. Within a year her confidence, and her reading ability, returned to normal because the 'learning gaps' had been filled and Jan felt confident that she was moving along with the main body of the class again. Don't dismiss the possibility of a reading disorder out of hand; but before you panic always look for common-sense practical reasons why your child's reading difficulty is occurring.

Sam also showed indications of dyslexia. A bright ten-year-old, with a tested reading age of seven years eight months, he was assigned two hours' extra teaching one-to-one in school every week. Working with him alone for such a long time, his teacher had the opportunity to focus on his individual problems. She noticed that his mistakes were frequently those that would normally be expected from a very young child. His difficulties were caused not from a 'dyslexia', but simply because he had never learned to read properly. He could sometimes work out words from their context, but he obviously could not understand every word and he didn't know enough basic words automatically by sight or enough phonics to work out words that he had not experienced reading before. When she looked into Sam's history she realised for the first time that family circumstances had meant that he had moved to four different schools in three years and had simply lost track. Communication between home and school had been poor and the obvious reasons for Sam's problems hadn't come to light. He needed to go back to master all the basic skills of reading in a consistent way before he would be able to read comfortably again.

One of the most useful and effective methods of teaching a child who needs practice of phonics and rhyme is through the Phonological Awareness Training (PAT) Pack. This scheme is not a complete reading programme; rather, it teaches children to recognise the sound of individual phonemes. Designed for use in accompaniment with picture books, stories, and poems, PAT provides a clear, straightforward set of worksheets, reading lists, and sentence dictation sheets. By teaching a child these phonic building blocks, the method aims to enable him to deconstruct words and decipher a meaning from their component parts.

PAT doesn't offer a miracle cure. But it does provide a skilfully produced, well-organised schedule of work, free from the jargon that so often haunts many educational schemes. One of the great strengths of PAT is that it recognises that children need an enormous amount of one-to-one attention if they are to be helped effectively as individuals each with his own set of difficulties. If you can spare half an hour a day, the PAT programme is comprehensive, straightforward and well explained, and likely to be a great help.

Anyone who has spent much of his or her life teaching children to read first-hand will acknowledge that, regardless of the powerful social forces at work, there undoubtedly remain specific learning difficulties, which require specific educational support. If your child can be given this teaching at his own school, where he is otherwise happy and stable, the effects of the problem will be minimised. Try not to be panicked into sending any child to a fee-paying school for dyslexics without thoroughly investigating all the options.

Remember that once you start paying for a child to go to a particular school his education will be very disrupted if financial pressures force you to take him out of the school. The British Dyslexia Association produces clear information which can be obtained from the address at the back of this book. Should your child prove dyslexic, expert help is also available through the state system, although getting the depth of expert assessment and teaching your child needs through his normal school can sometimes be a long, tedious and occasionally obscure process. Of course, all children react differently, but your child will probably feel happier working in familiar surroundings with the comfort of his present circle of friends than he would transferring to a specialist school.

If you suspect your child suffers from dyslexia, ask for him to be assessed by an educational psychologist – a free process which will take some months to arrange. If your child is diagnosed as being handicapped by a specific learning difficulty, or SpLD, appropriate help will be arranged for him and in cases where a child has a very severe language difficulty it can mean placement in a specialist school. But this is only judged necessary in very few cases so you need to work together with your child's teacher to help to develop study strategies that are particularly appropriate for his needs.

4

What Is 'Literacy'?

The word 'literacy' is, in many ways, a more fluid term than we would wish. While UNESCO, in 1965, defined a literate person as one who had acquired the knowledge and skills with written language demanded for an effective functioning within the community – and thereby limited literacy to those who had already had a number of years' schooling – it seems plain that, in fact, a level of literacy is implicit within all children even before primary school education begins. Models for testing literacy are frequently unsuccessful in younger children, simply because they are formulated to measure levels of literacy beyond their means.

As I shall show, a principal way in which you can aid your child's literacy levels occurs early, at pre-primary and primary school ages. By establishing and isolating your child's literacy difficulties early on, profound problems will be avoided later. One of the cardinal faults in present approaches to literacy stems from the fact that many – both teachers and parents – adhere too closely to what have been called 'literacy myths'. Although many of these popular conceptions about literacy contain at least a kernel of truth, any belief that literacy levels depend solely on sociological factors serves, to some extent, to create its own statistics and be a self-fulfilling prophecy.

Of course, initial literacy problems may be based on specific neurological or physical difficulty. It is important, if you feel that your child has trouble with literacy at an early stage, to isolate these factors. Good physical health is vital for good mental health. Even physical difficulties which you might think entirely unrelated to questions of literacy can have a profound influence upon a young child. Frequently, children with learning difficulties are found to have a history of bronchitis, asthmatic conditions, minor heart conditions, or other sicknesses. While these illnesses may be to an extent psychological, they also have a profound mental effect upon a child. An individual with physical difficulties will inevitably be more prone to nervous problems, and less able to learn quickly and ably than a healthy child. It is essential that any child attempting the struggle towards literacy should be provided with adequate physical care for her personal needs.

Some physical difficulties have a more specific influence on literacy. Any previously unnoticed sight or hearing troubles, as I have already discussed, can significantly hinder the progress of an otherwise able child. Any awkwardness in motor-functioning can also disrupt the learning process. Such problems may show up obviously through specific physical symptoms, such as uncoordinated or awkward movement, and involuntary tics or spasms. But they may be more subtle. As we have seen, difficulties in muscle control of the eye can in certain instances lead to considerable problems with the physical process of tracking text – problems which may have gone unnoticed in everyday activities.

But there are many instances where basic physical and neurological difficulties cannot explain literacy problems. Sometimes, these can be caused by flaws in teaching methods. One of the most popular theories relating to reading, in recent years, has been the belief that there is a specific age range during which children are particularly capable of both acquiring literacy and of learning language. Noam Chomsky, arguing that the language instinct is far more ingrained than is commonly supposed, asserted that all children possessed an innate linguistic ability, 'wired in' to the brain and enabling them to grasp rules of grammar at a certain age instinctively.

If it were the case that children at a certain age were fundamentally more attuned to the process of learning literacy, there would obviously be strong cause to argue that literacy learning should fundamentally be focused upon this age range, rather than any other. For many years, applying this argument, teachers believed that far from being beneficial it was actually harmful to introduce children to reading at too early an age. As Rudolph Steiner suggested that formal reading should not begin until the age of seven, so many other people in the first half of the twentieth century advocated a similar position.

But the argument is hard to accept at face value when the experts disagree among themselves on key features of it. The age judged to be the beginning of the period of 'reading readiness' has varied considerably from source to source. In 1965, Glen Doman advocated that reading should begin as early as two, in his book *Teaching Your Baby to Read*. Using the method of flash-cards, he attempted to show how even very young children would benefit from a systematic scheme aimed at improving literacy. Such arguments appealed to many people, but have failed to stand up after years of trying to put them into practice. Indeed, evidence has recently suggested that language learning is in fact easier for children of a later age group. McLaughlin, in 1977, showed that the capacity for foreign language learning was higher in older children than younger – as he stated: 'Controlled studies comparing younger children with older children generally indicated that older children performed better.'

But there are obvious problems about how you interpret this work. The fact that older children are more successful when faced with foreign language learning might not suggest that they are more adept at acquiring skills of literacy. In my view it rather demonstrates that a child who has already been provided with a framework of language and literacy, within a sound grasp of her mother tongue, finds it easier to apply known frameworks to other languages than an individual for whom the entire process of language and literacy is an alien one.

The notion of an age of initiation, and the belief that children of a certain age are inherently more inclined towards literacy than those of other ages, is a contentious one. In many regards it is another self-fulfilling prophecy, because such beliefs inevitably incline the individual towards educating a child at the age which they judge to be apt. If the child then learns to read, that is taken as 'proof' that the method works. But if you look at all the variations on this theme, all that is really proven is that children can learn to read at a wide variety of ages. It is certainly true that in some contexts theories relating to age initiation have produced dramatic results. Within Steiner education, for example, children who are encouraged into literacy only at seven, having developed a variety of creative skills prior to this age, would argue that such a system owes more to inherently superior modes of education, especially the small number of pupils per teacher, than to any particular age limitations placed upon that education. In an environment such as that propounded by Steiner – in which children are granted considerable individual attention and care – education in general, including literacy, will inevitably flourish.

As we have seen, in the battle towards literacy much still depends on a variety of preconceptions which can serve to hinder, rather than help, the individual child. Perhaps the most powerful example of the influence which preconceptions can have upon a child was demonstrated by Rosenthal and Jacobson, in 1968. In their study *Pygmalion in the Classroom*, teachers were encouraged to isolate and concentrate on particular pupils. These pupils, they had been informed by the psychologists, were significantly gifted and were to be encouraged. Although in fact the children were in no way more or less gifted than many of their contemporaries, Rosenthal and Jacobson showed that the simple fact of a teacher being made to believe these individuals were particularly capable led them to undergo considerable academic improvement. In a later experiment, in 1976, teachers who had been told normal children were suffering from a specific learning difficulty reported considerable problems in the work of those observed. Others, who had not been given this misinformation, recorded no such problems. Evidently, then, a child's ability is significantly affected by the preconceptions of those around them. (And as an aside, I would stress that both as a teacher and as a parent I have deep moral reservations about experiments like these, involving children who were in no sense voluntary guinea-pigs.)

If a child's ability is affected by the perceptions of others, it would seem that misconceptions created by sociological influences increase with age. At the age of five, a child is relatively unaware of any learning discrepancies between her and her contemporaries. But, as we have already seen, the feeling of isolation engendered by literacy difficulties begins the moment a child becomes aware that she is in some way abnormal. In time, without sufficient guidance and assistance, even a child who begins her academic career experiencing relatively minor learning difficulties will come to associate literacy with shame and awkwardness – in turn, her problems will inevitably increase.

The 'Literacy Hour' expounded by the UK Department for Education and Employment in 1998 goes some way towards minimising literacy problems in school. By allocating an hour a day solely to literacy, throughout primary education, the government aims to reduce such difficulties. This hour utilises a variety of teaching methods to build a cohesive knowledge of the fundaments of literacy. Within a combination of shared class work and individual study, it is hoped that children will learn to grasp a variety of literacy skills.

Such a scheme should create considerable benefits within the class as a whole. But, with its emphasis upon class teaching rather than one-to-one specialist tuition, the methods – like any which focus upon a class as a whole – inevitably mean that those children with limited reading skills are to some extent excluded. Although these methods should ensure that literacy for most children shows a marked improvement, there will be some who simply cannot maintain effective progress in class.

Children with reading difficulties thrive on individual attention. Assessment of their own needs and problems, coupled with a teaching programme tailored to these particular requirements, is almost certain to be beneficial. There are very effective schemes of work which can be used to teach children who find getting to grips with reading hard. In the remainder of this chapter I aim to outline the most efficient schemes which may be used in specialist tuition. They do, to some extent, represent an ideal; nevertheless, it is to be hoped that they will be used increasingly within our educational system.

As in ordinary medicine and health, when it comes to literacy problems, prevention is better than cure. The most effective way to assist any individual with literacy problems is by catching those problems almost before they begin. The most successful scheme detailing early limitation of reading difficulties in use today was first propounded by Professor Dame Marie Clay, of New Zealand. In the introduction to her book *The Early Detection of Reading Difficulties*, Clay states: 'My research question in 1962 was "Can we see the process of learning to read going wrong, close to the onset of reading instruction?" The answer was "Yes".'

Clay argues that initial reading difficulties can frequently be simply and systematically rectified. A child who is made aware early on of an easy method of reading will inevitably carry that method with her throughout her academic career. And it doesn't matter what it is, as long as it works for that child. In contrast, an individual who develops reading difficulties quickly compounds these difficulties through familiarity. The process of reading rapidly becomes automatised, to the extent that individuals come to observe complex syntactical cues without conscious effort; likewise, any mistakes developed early on will soon become bad habits inherent to the reading process of a problem reader. This leads to the situation, encountered in any school, of significant literacy discrepancies between contemporaries. Indeed, by the fourth year of schooling, a teacher will have to assist with a variety of children whose literacy abilities stretch over a nominal range of five years – covering both retarded and gifted readers. According to Clay, the basis for reading difficulties which leads to such extreme discrepancies is founded on young children developing and accepting reading systems of their own which are at fault within the first years of their academic career. These defects must be caught early – they become habituated when practised for as little as twelve to eighteen months.

The most essential aspect of special needs teaching, then, and the most effective, should occur as soon as problems become apparent. Clay's system, now applied throughout New Zealand, was to enforce a diagnostic survey of all children after only one year of tuition. This survey aims to pinpoint particular problems and work against them before they can become ingrained as the accepted norm for an individual child.

This is not to say that Clay does not believe literacy can be helped outside a school environment. Successful reading and writing begins, like so many other things, in those impressionable years before school. A good pre-school exposure to the mechanics of a country's language obviously helps further learning.

Whatever a child's pre-school literacy level, on beginning formal education she should have the benefit of a good literacy curriculum that takes into account her particular needs. The early intervention schemes and programmes expounded by Clay involve precise attention to each child. Individually tailored lessons, which are carefully designed to help children with problems in reading, spelling or writing, can allow a child to reach the average standards required remarkably quickly. In *Reading Recovery – A Handbook for Teachers in Training*, Clay ably and succinctly propounds her scheme for early detection of reading difficulties. This relies on three cardinal principles:

1 a check on the age group at the end of the first year of school
2 a second-chance programme for those who need it
3 specialist services for those very few whose problems persist after the intervention

A key component of this approach is the idea that a child with literacy problems will find herself hindered, rather than assisted, when forced to learn at a level higher than that which she finds comfortable. An individual presented with texts carefully collated for her own special needs will read those texts contentedly; one presented with work beyond her literacy ability will falter, stall and even lose her previous capacities through lack of practice on more familiar texts.

Such a reading scheme logically demands considerable individual attention for problem children. It is impossible within the existing UK state system to apply this to all children; Clay observes that eighty to ninety per cent of children will require neither the programme itself, nor any modified version of it. But those who do require the scheme will show radically and significantly improved literacy levels when educated in the one-on-one manner which she suggests.

Remedial teaching has made great strides but along with radical improvements there has been a considerable influx of misconstrued or misinterpreted beliefs about reading difficulties. We have already seen how this can lead to children with more superficial problems finding themselves saddled with the terminology of dyslexia, or other neurological disorders. Such conditions really do exist, but they are not as widespread as many accounts would have you believe, and their effects can be minimised much more easily than you might think.

In order to obtain an accurate Diagnostic Survey, Clay argues, it is sensible to ascertain reading levels in three principal ways:

1 by considering the child's reading ability with the text she is currently studying
2 by considering her ability when faced with a harder text
3 by observing her strengths with relation to easier and earlier texts

In this way it is possible to build up a composite picture of the weaknesses in a child's reading. Perhaps more important is the freedom to focus upon that child's particular strengths. Praising strengths is always a more productive approach to teaching than hammering away at weaknesses.

For beginner readers it is generally fairly easy to ascertain accurately a particular reading level. Clay suggests that a simple system be applied rapidly to obtain awareness both of a child's current level of literacy and of her progress. In reading with a child, she observes, it is important to measure her successes and failures intimately. When she is successful with a word, she suggests, her teacher or helper should mark that word with a tick. Failures to decipher words should in turn be marked with a cross. If a line or sentence is omitted, all words within that sentence are automatically regarded as errors in reading.

Clay advocates a reinforcement of texts with which the pupil feels reasonably comfortable. The reading level of a child may be accurately ascertained by calculating her error rate with any particular text. If this rate is over ten per cent it means she is trying to read a text she finds too difficult. Such ambitious attempts can only serve to hinder a child's progress. Problems with particular texts render a child less able to judge whether her efforts are good or bad – this in turn diminishes the value of reading. Any child must learn to predict from the baseline of her own expectations, and these expectations are formed from her experience of the written word. A child who is given a text which does not conform to these expectations will find herself stripped of the clues which she needs to make her a successful reader – without these, no individual can readily understand or learn text.

To read any continuous text, an individual must rely on

a variety of complex and inter-balanced skills. Obviously, weaknesses in a particular area of literacy must inevitably lead to flaws in reading skills. More surprisingly, specific strengths – especially when coupled with weaknesses – can also hinder a child's reading development. An example of this occurs when a child is particularly strong at oral skills. One who read with the fluency of well-developed oral language can be less successful at understanding what is being read than another who struggles with text, yet ultimately, with much self-correction, arrives at a truer interpretation. A fast reader can be one who is taking little visual account of text – who relies upon oral skills over those specifically required for reading. In maintaining fluency, yet failing to notice errors, such a reader will form patterns of reading which, if unchecked, can cause considerable difficulties later on.

In the early stages of literacy, then, it is particularly necessary to determine the personal clues which a child uses to interpret text. A child with good oral skills will often read a version which, while different from that on the page, is grammatically correct and coherent. One possessed of more limited oral skills will find forming or deciphering grammatical sentences more difficult. Frequently, a principal fault among children with poor grammatical awareness can be that, while they are as capable of deciphering individual words as many contemporaries, they have considerable trouble placing these words in a comprehensible order. One of the essential aspects of Clay's system is the stress which it places on the fact that reading is very intimately related to speaking. As such, it is often helpful to ask a child with poor reading skills to reread texts which she has dictated as her own. By rereading her own stories, a child will be utilising systems of speech which she has already developed. Freed from the strain of having to decipher and understand grammatical systems other than hers, she will in turn be more able to focus on the written word.

Sometimes a child's reading difficulties will be linked with simple errors which, through their sheer simplicity, have previously gone unchecked. Many children have literacy problems which are seated in the very fundaments of reading. A thorough comprehension of the alphabet is obviously essential to good literacy – if you are worried about your child's reading, it is important both to stress and to test her alphabet awareness. In addition, many conventions about language which a reader comes automatically to regard as the norm are in fact entirely arbitrary, and can cause considerable confusion for individuals who have failed to grasp them. Use of punctuation and capital letters, and even more simple concepts such as the definition of a letter and a word, can make for great and persistent difficulties. It is frequently surprising how much trouble a problem reader has with these simple concepts; in turn, a good awareness of them can make for a powerful and rapid improvement in literacy.

The diagnostic survey which Clay says should be applied following the first year of tuition serves to describe a child's strengths and weaknesses in reading. Using this system, failures in location, text placing and language are isolated and may be worked upon. The first year at school is, in many regards, the most important academic year of your child's life. In *The Early Detection of Reading Difficulties*, Clay makes a pertinent analogy between the manner in which literacy is still taught and the way that the education of other subjects has changed drastically in recent years. The concept of learning as the simple acquisition of facts, she observes, is an outmoded one. In mathematics, or in the sciences, knowledge is now measured not just by the unchecked accumulation of information – it also relies on an awareness of the principles behind this information, and in the strategies required for these subjects. In a similar manner, Clay argues, when teaching a child to read it is essential to focus not on the effects of a literacy difficulty, but on the cause – on the misjudged strategies which a problem reader applies to a text.

The programme does not deny the reality of reading difficulties and disabilities. As Clay states:

Most children who had made little progress by 6 years are children who brought some limitation or handicap to school, who are going to carry that handicap with them and who are going to have to learn to read in spite of it [page 38].

Clearly her message is not that such difficulties do not exist; it is rather than these problems may be lessened, and in some cases even annulled, by prompt action which is specific to a child's needs. The concept that children may be divided easily into those who succeed and those who fail at literacy is an outmoded one. All children who are failures fail for their own specific reasons and can only be helped by careful focused attention upon their particular difficulties. It is the system that fails them, not the other way round.

Within most state systems, it had been traditionally held that remedial teaching was impracticable in the first few years of primary tuition. The logic of this stemmed from the belief that considerable and long-term reading difficulties were literally undetectable early on. Utilising coherent and cohesive evidence, Clay showed that this was not the case; that children as young as five or six could be accurately divided into good, average and problem readers – and that the problems could be solved.

The first steps in Clay's reading scheme are simple and

easily applied. As we have seen, much is concerned with finding a child's personal level of literacy and working alongside her capabilities. Texts which are overly easy will fail to stimulate and educate a child; those which are too complex will isolate and bewilder her. The most effective step towards a good literacy teaching is to establish, by careful tests, the most difficult text which your child can read while still maintaining a ninety per cent accuracy rating. Following this, new material and information may be introduced. It is essential at all times to focus upon your child's own problems – whether with grammar, sentence construction, or more simple skills concerned with text recognition.

At this stage, it is particularly vital that your child is not presented with a surplus of bewildering information. Be sure never to focus entirely upon her weaknesses. If a difficult task must be undergone, try to link this with other, easier skills which your child has already acquired. An important step towards bolstering confidence lies in providing a child with the means and capabilities to recognise her own errors. Encourage her to decipher words on her own wherever possible. When she has worked out problem texts, ask her how she did so. Often, even a child who has resolved a puzzle with reading remains uncertain how she arrived at the solution; enabling her to clarify her own thoughts remains at all times an essential element of good literacy teaching.

Clay's reading programme, then, requires immediate and intensive tuition for those children who fail in literacy at a basic level when tested at the age of six. Its plan of early intervention was aimed to accelerate a child's progress, and in turn to render that child as independent of special tuition as possible. The intensive tuition should be discounted wherever feasible, enabling a child to re-enter normal education. Using these notions of tuition, problem children were able to make rapid and considerable gains in literacy. Indeed, in the 'Reading Recovery Research Project' of 1978, Clay showed that problem children who were given this form of intensive personal assistance made gains which were significantly greater than those of others within their group. This is not to say that, at the end of the course of tuition, problem children had acquired as high or higher literacy levels than those for whom specialist tuition had not been judged necessary. Rather, throughout the period in which they were educated according to Clay's method, their literacy improved at a faster rate than that of ordinary children in a class context. They really did catch up.

Clay's methods work. Educationally significant gains were made by all children receiving individual tuition – gains which they would have been unable to make within a class environment. By isolating reading difficulties early, Clay succeeded in enabling many children who would otherwise have been saddled with the burden of literacy difficulties throughout their lives to succeed in a very short space of time. While the intensive tuition required for the first part of Clay's programme appears, superficially, to bring a costly financial burden upon the school system, realistically such immediate support can only serve to diminish financial outlay in later special needs tuition. It also has further huge long-term benefits – individuals who pass their exams will be more likely to succeed and more capable of avoiding unemployment.

The administrative alteration needed to underpin Clay's educational scheme is both simple and radical. Within the first year of education, she argues, all schools should attempt to ensure that every one of their pupils is given at least two hours of personal tuition each week. Such tuition will serve to isolate particular difficulties; if necessary, these will be lessened or annulled by closer individual supervision.

A typical Reading Recovery lesson conforming to Clay's plan will be highly organised and extremely intensive. Importantly, it will also never lose track of the fact that, to ensure good teaching, it is essential that a child finds a lesson both informative and enjoyable. An example lesson might involve a child revising a number of words, and begin with reading sessions which specifically choose texts the child has already read, and feels comfortable and familiar with. Following this, the child will read the most recent book she has studied in class. The first two weeks of these classes will rely upon texts with which the child has already acquired a familiarity. By re-asserting known texts, confidence is built and existing knowledge strengthened.

The closing phase of the lesson scheme relies upon the introduction of new text to the child. Prior to the process of reading, this text will be familiarised to the child in every way possible. She will be made aware of the characters of the book, its pictures and the story-lines it deals with. Finally, she will be encouraged to read, with her teacher's support. At this point, a child will be encouraged also to read books at home, on her own or with her family. In this way, confidence is built and a child should develop into an independent and autonomous reader.

In 1993, OFSTED (Office of Standards in Educational Development) published a report titled *Reading Recovery in New Zealand*. This report chronicled the achievements of Clay's scheme and speculated whether such a method might be equally beneficial within the British school system. Its conclusions were positive, and the same year saw experiments with Early Intervention special needs tuition begin in Great Britain. In February 1995, the School Curriculum and Assessment Authority published its findings concerning this first cohesive study of the system in Britain. Covering more than

400 children from varied sociological backgrounds, the programme prescribed modes of teaching which were in many
ways radically similar to that which had reaped such profound benefits in the New Zealand system. By the age of
six, those children possessed of early reading difficulties were
involved in early intervention schemes consisting of similar
intensive teaching methods.

The Early Intervention method utilised in this experiment
owes much to Clay's reading philosophy; however, it is also
part of a general trend towards earlier remedial teaching.
Wasik and Slavin (1993) formed one of the most recent sur-
veys of the effects of one-to-one remedial teaching on very
young children. This survey, conducted in a variety of Ameri-
can States, focused upon five separate systems of early
remedial tuition. It found considerable gains could be made
with each and every one.

This was not to say that each of these systems was of equal
benefit to remedial children. Ultimately, the most effective
modes of teaching were found to be those which focused
upon a wide variety of methods, rather than being reliant
upon intensive education of a particular element of literacy.
Significantly, the most considerable successes were found
within those schemes where particular stress had been placed
upon phoneme education. In every instance, children were
shown to be more successful – both in class and in remedial
instruction – when emphasis was placed upon phonic awareness. Phonemes, remember, are the units of sound, represented by letters and groups of letters (graphemes).

Within the British scheme, those selected as suffering reading difficulties were withdrawn from class for individual
tuition – a process which took half an hour daily. Much as
in Clay's method, children were initially to build confidence
with familiar texts, and in two weeks were encouraged to

read other, unfamiliar books. The average number of weeks which any child spent upon the programme was sixteen; following further difficulties, those who had failed to reach an average level of literacy would then be referred to a remedial service.

Clay's Reading Recovery system showed dramatic results within the first year. Children educated in accordance with this scheme made, on average, seventeen months of normal progress in the nine months in which the scheme was applied. After it ended, the children who had participated in the Reading Recovery programme continued to show considerable progress over a control group of other remedial children who had not participated. But the gulf between the two groups gradually lessened, and one full school year later these children demonstrated only six months' improvement on the control remedial group. Nevertheless, this improvement is noteworthy when it applies to children of this young age. Furthermore, most teachers agreed that the simple process of participating in the Reading Recovery scheme led to the establishment of new, superior modes of literacy teaching in the classroom; so the 'control group' itself benefited from the scheme to an extent.

Clay's scheme has much to offer and also creates an improvement throughout the other members of the class. The methods propounded by the Reading Recovery scheme, when infiltrated into normal class teaching, show improvements which, while less considerable than those caused by one-to-one teaching, were nevertheless significant. But Reading Recovery demanded sixty minutes of one-to-one teaching every week. Inevitably, this means that the financial outlay for the Reading Recovery method was unusually high – approximately three times more expensive than conventional alternatives.

The considerable costs of the Reading Recovery scheme owe much to its concentrated form; but, as we have seen, they lead to minimised outlay in special needs teaching throughout the remainder of a child's academic career. The initial great outlay, however, has inevitably meant that it has been only partially accepted in the curriculum of Great Britain. While there have been a few limited successful trials of this scheme in Britain, the methods have yet to be taken up wholesale.

The Literacy Hours approach is likely to help most children to read happily and successfully. Some children, though, will inevitably still fall through the net, because their specific reading difficulties require individual attention. Children who start to learn to read formally within the system of a Literacy Hour will have fewer problems than those who have come to this scheme after they have already been learning to read by various methods for several years.

There are few teachers in Britain skilled in teaching Reading Recovery, as the training is demanding and intensive. But some schools offer holiday courses in reading which embody some of the principles of Clay's method. These are by no means offered by every school and are usually confined to boosting the reading abilities of children as they move from primary to secondary education. The courses are very beneficial to children – not simply because of the teaching methods used, but also because teachers are able to deal with each child's reading problems with a level of individual attention. Although Reading Recovery has to be supervised by a trained teacher, the parent is encouraged to play a supportive role, providing assistance and encouragement. If your child is offered one it can be immensely beneficial.

5

Reading Difficulties in Adolescence

Although very few children reach their teenage years without learning to read at a basic, functional level, more minor reading difficulties can still cause study problems. Courses and classes in secondary education demand a level of literacy which a significant number of children do not feel comfortable with. Many are simply unable to read sufficiently quickly and effectively to deal with school work or examinations at this high level. While a child may be intelligent enough to fully understand sophisticated theories and ideas, if he can't handle the reading level demanded by his relevant course books he is prevented from learning effectively.

A young person with poor reading skills may communicate well, and cope easily with tests based on speaking and listening; but almost all exams rely on a student's capacity to read, write and remember. Background reading is obviously essential in secondary education where the relevant section of a set course book is often the basis of the lesson and the homework generated by it. Reading problems, which make understanding course books a puzzle, coupled with lack of organisation and motivation, are the basis of most of the learning difficulties experienced by children facing exams. As well as making background reading stressful, inadequate and unproductive, reading difficulties will inevitably make it harder to produce coherent notes in lesson time.

Following through a course of study for an exam without having clear memorable notes is next to impossible. The simplest and most effective way to minimise note-taking problems and stress is to use a tape-recorder. Recorded learning sessions can be listened through at home and notes taken in a relaxed way. There is the added advantage that difficult sections of the lesson can be replayed over and over again until they become clear and fall into place. Some computer users can type so efficiently that they can transfer words almost simultaneously from tape to screen. Working through the finished typescript later, spell-checking or just reading through, does a lot to set facts in place and make the intended learning structure of the lesson more comprehensible. Although some teachers may feel uncomfortable about their lessons being taped, most will generally relent once they know that the tape-recorder is really necessary for that particular student. Research notes for course work projects can also be worked out on tape and then put on to computer. But organisation is vitally important: tapes need to have their contents clearly labelled. If you can help your child to type or write out the major points of each lesson that he has on tape in simple, straightforward words this can be a real help to learning and later to exam revision.

Teenage readers working towards exams have to learn how to find and use information relevant to their study topics. Although computers have done much to make the search for relevant facts quicker and less complicated, printout still needs to be read and understood. Finding facts about a particular subject may be relatively straightforward but many inexperienced readers are forced into panic when they realise that they have to use their source material to produce a clear and concise written argument. Many students are very stressed by the difficulty that they find reading and understanding source material, often assuming that they are expected to provide all the information required for complex essays and exams primarily from their own thoughts. They do not realise that books are there to help.

Young people who have always found reading a struggle often feel hostile towards books and have little idea how to use a library effectively. Spend time showing your child how to find and use information. Show him how to use a CD Rom and if he finds reading troublesome get him a CD designed for a younger reader. This may not have everything he needs but what relevant information it does contain will be accessible and he will be able to understand and use it confidently. Show him how getting facts and opinions from books is a help to clarifying his own opinions rather than just a way of regurgitating what other people know and think.

Children need to learn how to structure their thoughts. One common feature among retarded readers is the fear of making a mistake – which in turn inhibits progress. Many retarded readers are characterised by reaching a particular, simple reading level, and staying there – fearing the errors that all progress must inevitably bring. Any individual will be less inclined to read if he feels these mistakes will be condemned. By demonstrating to your child that it is only through his mistakes that he can be assisted to learn, you can encourage him to read texts which he would otherwise fear.

With children who are retarded readers, rather than possessed of further learning difficulties, much of the problem is caused by previous negative associations with reading. As such, many difficulties can be overcome by allowing your child a wider, though still structured, control over his reading material and the reading process in general. This is particularly important for older readers. Such readers will benefit if you explain the course to them; they may also benefit by being provided with a reasoned assessment of their own reading skills, coupled with suggestions on the manner in which they could be improved. The pupil who assists in forming his own goals, with the aid of a parent or teacher, will be far more eager to work towards a target he is confident he can eventually, with time and patience, reach.

As well as enabling your child to play an active part in expressing his views, it can be of enormous benefit if you strive to help him relay his views in the most effective manner possible. This can apply to ascertaining his own opinions concerning his course teaching and his particular needs; it can also apply to showing him the correct ways to arrange his written work. Encourage him, when considering a subject or argument, to propound views both for and against it, in a reasoned list. Freed from the demanding constraints of an essay format, many children with learning difficulties find it considerably easier to pin-point coherent and cogent arguments. It is often a great liberation for a child when he is made aware that, rather than blindly listing and categorising facts, he is free – and indeed encouraged – to present these facts in accordance with his own personal argument.

Young people who have not read a great deal often make the naïve assumption that whatever is written in textbooks concerning their subjects must be both true and relevant. A helpful exercise for those disillusioned with books can be to explain where past tests went wrong. Show your child that at one time books were written in praise of slavery, or that women were once judged in written texts to be inferior to men. A knowledge that books can be mistaken will bring considerable confidence to a child uncertain of his own argument, in the light of disagreement from written texts.

If a child with literacy problems is compelled to undergo a written exam, his work will inevitably not be an accurate mirror of his knowledge. In order to minimise these problems, encourage your child to explain ideas to you cogently and simply. When he has obtained a clear understanding through oral communication, he should find that writing about the subject becomes easier. Many exams are failed not just through ignorance, but rather by a fear of reading and writing which can be overcome with practice.

The literacy strategies outlined in this chapter are useful allies in the struggle for learning, even for an older child who finds reading a dull and difficult experience. However, many strategies do assume that a child possesses at least a reasonable level of literacy, and is able to understand and interpret written questions. In certain circumstances, a child's literacy can be so poor that – while skilled in practical work – he will prove unable to decipher written exam papers. If this is the case, it can be possible for your child to work separately in examinations, consulting a teacher when necessary. Most exam boards should agree to this in the case of a student with a specific learning difficulty, although the precise rules concerning this process vary considerably across the exam boards. Never assume that you can, or cannot, obtain help in any given position – always ask. If your child is ultimately unable to obtain the benefit you feel he requires, remember that schools and colleges must work strictly within a system outlined by their examination board.

In *Diagnosing Dyslexia* (The Basic Skills Agency) Cynthia Klein observes:

Examination Boards, Higher Education Institutions, and professional bodies usually make various provisions for students with specific learning difficulties, primarily of

107

extra time and sympathetic consideration for spelling, handwriting, and written expression difficulties.

Such provisions may be used in most circumstances; inevitably, they do not extend to English examinations. In order for your child to obtain this assistance, GCSE and A Level boards require the report of an educational psychologist – although sometimes an educational psychologist's accompanying letter with a trained learning-support tutor's report may be judged acceptable. Consult your school's learning-support tutor concerning your child's personal needs; where necessary, they should provide your child an appointment with an educational psychologist.

Even if your child is unable to obtain this form of academic assistance, he will be considerably aided by your own time and by a variety of revision methods designed for his personal literacy needs. While it is not realistic to expect that written text can be entirely ignored in the preparation for exams, this text can be amply and ably embellished by other sources. Tape-recorded notes, and relevant tapes and video-cassettes are a great way to revise, and of particular use should your child be learning languages. But any course will benefit from the use of outside sources – a cassette eagerly listened to will inevitably be of more worth than text reluctantly read.

One of the strongest defences against fear of illiteracy in exams is familiarity. Gary was good at graphic design, yet failed his mock exam by being unable to read the paper correctly. Following this, by practice and repetition with past papers, his teacher demonstrated the similarities in structure found between various questions. Obtaining past exam papers, and reading through them clearly with your child, can be a powerful way to allay exam fears.

Encourage your child to make reasoned and ordered notes.

Children with reading difficulties often find it far easier to present a spoken argument than one which is written; if this is the case, suggest they tape-record their thoughts and make written notes later. If your child is having difficulties with his school work it is important to consider whether his problems lie not with the actual work content, but with the manner in which it is presented. A child may appear intelligent and vocal in class, yet have little comprehension of course texts. I recall a colleague experiencing considerable problems with an individual pupil who frequently either refused to complete his homework, or produced work which failed to conform with her instructions. When his problem was investigated, his teacher found that he had trouble actually understanding the course book. Startled by this discovery, she proceeded to rewrite the course book every week in a more readily comprehensible manner.

In doing so, Mark's teacher made use of what is known as the SMOG ready reckoner. This system provides a method of calculating the reading level of books and magazines. By simplifying the text, she found not only that Mark made good progress, but that her pupils as a whole became more successful in class. What she had seen before as problems in the comprehension of complex ideas were, she realised, more about difficulties in interpretation of the written word.

The SMOG ready reckoner is superficially complex and may be difficult to grasp immediately. In establishing the reading level of any text, this method suggests that ten consecutive sentences should be taken from it. Within these sentences, the number of words with more than three syllables should be added; the end result should then be multiplied by three. Having done this, the final result will be closest to one of the following numbers:

1 4 9 16 25 36 49 64 81 100 121 144 169

Take the square root of the number which is closest to your own and finally add eight. This will leave you with the SMOG reading level of your text. The level which the average reader is meant to understand readily and easily – and that at which middle-of-the-range newspapers are pitched – is 10 (the SMOG index for this book is slightly higher, about 11 or 12).

Should you be working with only one individual, the principle behind the SMOG system is much easier. Simply read through a chosen text with that person, noting when and where he fails with particular words. If he is finding trouble understanding five words on each normally spaced page of a typical school story book (approximately 200 words), this indicates that he is attempting a text which is above his reading level.

It is important to remember that many older students who find difficulty in reading are otherwise as capable of absorbing complex information as any of their classmates. Any attempt to educate a fifteen-year-old with reading difficulties, using text designed to conform to the interests of a younger age group, can only serve to enhance his sense of isolation and embarrassment. In order to avoid this problem, it is possible to obtain a series of reading books suitable for older readers which are written using a level of language appropriate for individuals with basic reading skills (some examples are given at the end of this book). These books will enable your child to enjoy reading works which, although utilising simple text, contain the interests of his own age group.

Michael was a teenager who found considerable difficulty accepting his reading problems. Rather than take part in reading activities which led to him feeling left out and embarrassed, he would frequently sit silently with his closed class book on his desk, gazing abstractedly out of the window. Although Michael himself showed little interest in reading, his ambition to become a mechanic would inevitably demand a higher level of literacy than he had attained.

The sense of humiliation experienced by Michael in class meant that he was inevitably most effectively aided in a one-to-one situation. But the lack of interest caused by his feelings of embarrassment was compounded by a sincere disregard for the texts which he had been offered to aid his reading difficulties. By talking with him, his learning-support teacher was able to establish that he had always despised the simple fiction books which he was assigned within class. Understandably, he found considerably more interest in texts which conformed with his personal ambitions. To maintain Michael's interest, his teacher began to ask him to read texts which he found both entertaining and useful. Suggesting that she required a car for herself, she asked Michael to help her in searching for one suited to a teacher with a low income – studying car magazines and manuals carefully.

Using this method, Michael's reading improved satisfactorily. Confident that he knew more about cars than his teacher, he found that this enabled him to regard her as his equal. There was little shame in asking her to aid him in deciphering text – particularly when his personal knowledge could help her own interests. By focusing upon those which complied with Michael's personal interests and ambitions, she was able to demonstrate the importance of reading for furthering these ambitions.

When encouraging your teenage child to read, it is important to remember that he will respond most effectively to being treated as an equal. Ask him to aid or advise in areas where he is likely to be better informed – in computing, for example. The feeling that he is assuming a confident and beneficial role is a powerful incentive to any individual when attempting to learn a task he finds difficult and purposeless. I remember working with a student who suffered extreme problems learning facts which he regarded as unnecessary. A keen football fan, he found geography considerably more interesting when applied to the relevant soccer teams of countries and cities.

Some teenagers, as we have seen, are unwilling to read, write or research unless they feel that their efforts have a specific reference to their own lives. Perhaps the most inspiring instance of this I have encountered was in the case of Dean and Grant. Having suffered extreme literacy problems, this pair were readily dismissed as non-readers. When they learned that their local football pitch was threatened with closure, though, they decided to produce their own project demonstrating public and personal reasons why it should stay.

Although these attempts were initially awkward, with perseverance they were prompted into putting together a carefully collated and reasoned project. Collecting information from friends, they produced an impressive feature which the school, and later even the local newspapers, were eager to print.

Most teenagers with poor reading skills are boys – individuals who at this age would far rather be seen to be offering their own help and support than receiving it from others. Finding texts which conform to their own interests – and expressing a wish to learn more about these interests yourself – is a powerful first step towards making anyone interested in reading. I once worked with two teenage boys who resolutely refused to read. This struggle against reading became a battle between the two of them to be the first to read when I unwittingly produced a book about their special interest. Unknown to me, each had a pet hamster at home, and they were delighted when I brought a book about hamsters into school. They were understandably eager to learn more, and to share their knowledge with me and each other.

As we have seen, it is frequently the case that pupils with good practical skills fail exams in practical subjects through literacy difficulties. Robert, for example, was an excellent sportsman. But his literacy problems were such that he was afraid he might fail his exams. An active individual, he found great difficulty settling to solitary study. Although his arguments in class seemed considered and well-advised, his written work appeared totally divorced from his normal conversation, and was rambling and uncertain.

Robert's difficulties abated to a large extent when his sports teacher, aware of his writing difficulties, began to ask him to provide weekly reports on sporting events of his choice. By helping his writing style, Robert's teacher ensured that these reports improved – as did Robert's overall literacy.

If you have access to a computer – or even a typewriter – placing a professional sheen upon your child's work will encourage his interests and lead to renewed self-respect. Although not all children can hope to attain publication in a local newspaper – like Dean and Grant – any individual will benefit from the confidence that good presentation can bring to his work. Pride in his efforts will be significantly bolstered by its appearance. Likewise, when your child knows how cohesively and coherently to demonstrate his arguments to others – perhaps using a computer and with your help – he will be free to utilise this ability in his own written presentations. One of the most vital problems in children with literacy difficulties is not that they have nothing to say – it is rather that they are prevented from expressing their own views by the very medium that should enable them.

A key reason that a child dismisses reading can be the sense of isolation that such private study demands. Perhaps unsurprisingly, many children who revile the private study required by reading will find far more contentment when working with others. This can comprise joint projects; it can also take the form of reading a play. Reading within a play provides a sense of importance and purpose – every individual is assigned his own specific role, with which he is required to identify, and relied upon by others within his group. This can lead to a sense of involvement and enthusiasm which many individuals cannot produce when faced with the less personal mode of other fiction.

If you wish to support your child's literacy by exploring plays with him, there are several series of popular plays which are specifically written for young people possessed of only basic reading skills (again, some examples are given at the back of this book). Even if you or your child is unwilling to read these simple works, most plays written in modern English are easier to decipher than much literature. This is in part because a good play must, necessarily, make use of an idiom far closer to that of everyday life. Further to this, any mistakes made in reading a play are easily absorbed within the work of a group.

Coupled to the difficulties many older boys find in accepting text specifically designed for younger readers, some of them hold that reading should be regarded primarily as a female interest. Evidence suggests that in this they are, at least to a certain extent, correct. In Western societies reading is frequently presented as predominantly a female activity. Such texts as boys do find interest in show a marked difference from those presented for girls to enjoy. Magazines and comics designed for girls present stories or gossip in a simple narrative style; those favoured by boys utilise reading skills more relevant to newspapers or manuals, and in turn make profound use of sound effects to create a more sensory mode of interpretation. Dyslexia mainly affects boys. This may be principally because boys are by their very nature more uninterested in reading than girls. In 1975, Kennedy and Halinski observed: 'Females generally have been recognized by reading experts as being more interested in reading than males, as having a more positive attitude towards reading [page 521].'

However, there has been important evidence to suggest that these reading difficulties are frequently sociological. A survey of reading in Kent in the mid-1960s found no significant discrepancy in literacy levels between sexes. Logically, if these discrepancies owed nothing to sociological surroundings, one would expect there to be a greater level of conformity within varying studies than there actually is.

Working with any individual who finds reading difficult is an uphill struggle. In older readers, such problems are compounded by the fact that there can be a considerable feeling of humiliation associated with literacy trouble. Always respect a child's privacy; if he is willing to confide in you, he will feel an inevitable betrayal should he realise you are sharing his problems with other adults, or worse, with his contemporaries. It is a struggle for your child even to confide his problems to you – the discovery that you are betraying his trust can be a significant blow to his confidence.

Many older children find it difficult to acknowledge their reading problems even to their parents. To be stripped of the feeling of control, at a time when the need for control is becoming paramount, is to be deprived of confidence and laid open to embarrassment and, in the eyes of your child, humiliation. If your child feels this way, you have to respect his privacy, but there are courses of action you can take. One of the most effective modern ways of teaching older children to read – and a method which omits the need for outside help – is to use literacy boosting computer programmes. The use of these enables an individual to maintain control of his personal situation and to progress at a rate he finds comfortable without fear of embarrassment. There are many excellent literacy programs available and many more are being produced all the time (see details at the back of this book). If you are in any doubt as to which one to choose, consult the literacy specialist in your child's school; he or she will be glad to help, and should provide you with a programme conforming to both your child's needs and age range.

Older children with reading difficulties can find that they are confronted year after year with the same familiar, distinctly tedious texts. Paula was given a reading scheme repeatedly, yet made little progress. Her school, it seemed, had accepted the fact that this genial child had reading difficulties which would not be overcome. But by using a computer programme she rapidly found she was making progress, liberated both from the constraints of a particular scheme and from the fear of her friends' mockery.

Remember, twenty-five per cent of everything that we read, at a normal reading level, consists of just twelve words – 'a', 'it', 'of', 'he', 'that', 'I', 'the', 'in', 'to', 'is', 'and', 'was'. Further, our basic two hundred words compose seventy per cent of the average text. If an older child is having reading difficulties, ensure that his first step towards literacy is an awareness of these two hundred words – they can be found at the back of the book. And many find reading easier if they are free to assume an adult role – either in choosing their own text, or in aiding a younger child.

It is of course inevitable that some children will find reading an unfulfilling, mechanical exercise. Although these children

116

may be able and willing to learn the rudiments of literacy, it is at times necessary to accept that they will never take pleasure in the task. If this is the case, any child will be abetted by learning through listening, rather than reading. Attempt to find your child's course texts on tape or video; this will provide much-needed confidence and benefit his written work in turn. Reading problems cannot always be overcome – rather, they are frequently alleviated by the use of tapes or videos. Many children will also benefit from working in a group, with like-minded friends producing an essential stimulus that the written word cannot provide.

The ultimate message, then, when attempting to teach older children with reading difficulties – whether they are retarded readers, or suffer from a specific learning difficulty such as dyslexia – is that it is of cardinal importance to remember, at all times, that a child's self-esteem can frequently be linked with his reading difficulties. As we have seen, retarded readers are frequently by their nature disinclined to read texts with which they feel uncomfortable – texts which they believe will illuminate their faults. Early poor experiences with reading can often be compounded to make a child of average, or above-average, intelligence one with reading difficulties. Another problem is that it has become fashionable in recent years to blame the reading difficulties of many children upon emotional blocking.

Such a term is, by its very nature, a vague one. A child with no physical reason for a reading difficulty, who nevertheless forms an emotional block about reading, can find himself opposed to literacy for a variety of reasons. Such children may be possessed of a conscious, or unconscious refusal to learn, caused by one or more of the following stimuli:

1 Hostility towards parents, teachers, or a fellow sibling. In this context, a child may come to associate literacy with the individuals towards whom he feels hostile. As we have seen, this can frequently have a sexual basis – boys can, for example, dismiss reading as an essentially feminine task. If this is the case with your child, only constant reassurance of his personal strengths and capabilities can serve to demonstrate the use that literacy can have in his own life.

2 A feeling of resistance against the forceful insistence of either parents or teachers. If a child feels an excess of pressure towards a goal which he believes he is unable to attain, he will inevitably lose faith both in himself and in those setting the tasks. Over-zealousness, particularly when it is not linked with consideration concerning your child's own particular needs, can be one of the strongest barriers against literacy.

3 Simple hyperactivity can be one of the principal physical reasons for reading difficulties. As we have seen, this hyperactivity can be put to good use by involving a child's other interests to the full in his struggle for literacy. Learning how significant good knowledge of reading and writing can be in all aspects of modern life is often the only way to persuade a child entirely uninterested in literature that literacy will be of benefit to him.

4 Certain children will fear the maturity that literacy can bring them. Coming to associate literacy with maturity, they may consciously or unconsciously choose to remain infantile – to stay within the position which they have learned, from experience, enables them to attract the maximum level of attention. In such cases encouragement into literacy will be most effectively

brought about by demonstrating the strengths that it can bring.

Many children whose reading problems are based upon psychological, rather than neurological, premises come to acknowledge their reading difficulties as something to be accepted, rather than fought against. Such children characteristically demonstrate low drive in learning, coupled with only limited emotional expression. As we have seen, the emotional disturbance which results in these difficulties can be caused by processes (such as moving house) which many caring parents regard as insignificant, yet which can produce overwhelming reactions of fear and discomfort in a child. In such cases, attempting to fight literacy problems head-on may simply be a battle against the effects, rather than the causes of the crises that manifest themselves in literacy problems. If you suspect that your child's reading difficulties are predominantly emotionally based, talk through his personal fears with him; this can be the only way to enable a child to obtain the confidence necessary for a successful reader.

In addition, difficulties which do find their basis in a specific neurological problem – whether developmental dyslexia, or a more severe disability – will inevitably be lessened by close contact with your child's emotional fears and troubles. If the concept of dyslexia itself is one which causes considerable debate among psychologists, it seems clear that our only conclusion upon this subject can be to assert, in line with the Isle of Wight study of Michael Rutter and his colleagues mentioned in chapter three, that there are plainly one or more neurological conditions decidedly distinct from mere slow learning which can cause otherwise able children to experience difficulties with literacy. This is not to say that the word 'dyslexia' does not, perhaps, cover a wide variety of

119

sub-groups whose specific needs must be attended to in very particular ways. It has been argued that there are as many dyslexias as there are dyslexics. What must be asserted is that the concept of dyslexia, with its fashionable status, can do much to hinder a child who is a slow reader for other reasons, whether emotional, psychological or neurological. What must be conceded is that the concept of dyslexia – although at present an uncertain one which is misapplied in many cases – relates to a very real neurological condition which, as I have seen in my line of work, can be extremely troubling.

Ultimately, a teenager with literacy difficulties will inevitably experience crises linked with these problems to a greater degree than younger children. The burgeoning awareness of maturity, coupled with an encroaching fear that literacy may stay for ever outside his grasp, will inevitably cause any individual to experience disillusionment. For all the methods, principles and techniques which I have outlined, one core element remains paramount. In individuals of any age, and specifically in teenagers with reading difficulties, a sense of self-worth coupled to a prevailing belief that literacy remains possible will be of equal or more worth than any mechanically prescribed scheme or process. This applies to children whose reading difficulties are predominantly emotionally based; it carries equal weight with those whose problems have a more specific neurological basis. With help and encouragement, even individuals who regard reading as entirely alien can be encouraged towards improved literacy.

In the final chapter of this book we will be looking at the ways in which you can enable your child to obtain the best education available within the state system. Using the methods I shall be outlining, it should be possible to gain access to this system in the most satisfactory way for both you and your child. By applying these processes, in accordance with his specific personal needs, any individual should obtain the environment he requires to make the best of his reading skills, and in turn to make him a happier reader.

6

Working with the System

Although it has been subject to significant changes, the fundamentals of British special needs teaching have remained the same since the 1944 Education Act. This act binds all Local Education Authorities (LEAs) to an obligation to educate children in accordance with their age, ability and aptitude. It also sets an age range for special educational provision which has not altered – defining individuals aged between two and nineteen as entitled to this provision. The 1944 act defines eleven categories. According to this definition, an individual is entitled to special needs provision if she is blind, partially sighted, deaf, partially hearing, delicate, diabetic, epileptic, maladjusted, physically handicapped, aphasic, or educationally subnormal.

This precise categorisation of pupils with regard to their specific handicap rather than any personal need, was heavily criticised by a review group chaired by the moral philosopher Mary Warnock. Published in 1978, the Warnock Report expressed the philosophy that 'the purpose of education for all children is the same; the goals are the same but the help that individual children need in progressing towards them will be different'. The Warnock Report suggested in particular that the statutory categorisation of handicapped children be abolished, with every child being judged more specifically according to need. It was at this stage, also, that the five stages of progressive need were devised for children requiring special attention – categories which remain the backbone of much special needs teaching today, and which I will outline shortly.

The 1981 Education Act served to incorporate certain aspects of the Warnock Report. Principal among these was the establishment of the five stages of progressive need. Further to this, according to the act a child was defined as possessed of 'special educational needs' if she suffered a learning difficulty – either a physical disability or a significantly greater difficulty in learning than most children of the same age. After this act, the sole primary alteration to the education manifesto was made by the 1988 Education Reform Act. This requires all children to have access to a broad, balanced curriculum. The conditions of the Reform Act include most special needs students – only in particularly extreme cases may the curriculum be modified or ignored. The Warnock Report had shown that twenty per cent of all children required special needs help at some point in their academic career. The majority of this assistance would occur in the first three stages of the special needs programme – inside school, and within the framework of the National Curriculum.

In certain circumstances, as we have seen, children with particularly severe special needs may be exempted from all or part of the National Curriculum requirements. In such cases, exemption may be permanent, as we shall see. However, there are also more frequent occasions when a child's current needs require a temporary exemption from the straitened nature of the curriculum. These temporary exemptions occur either in the case of non-permanent sickness or trauma, when a head teacher believes a pupil's circumstances will change sufficiently within six months to permit the full

National Curriculum to be resumed; they also occur when the head teacher holds that an exemption will enable a more efficient assessment, and the establishment of a statement of special educational needs.

One of the principal problems leading to severe reading difficulties can be that within the state system children are often not subjected to high levels of expert assessment until it is too late. Although the state system can seem cruel in its impartiality, and in its failure to notice specific differences and difficulties between children early on, the vast majority of help that your child will obtain will probably come from within that system. Regardless of problems caused by class size, most teachers will notice reading problems that are specific to any child, and will be eager to work with her parents towards solving these difficulties. At the time of writing, all state schools are by law regulated by the Code of Practice outlined by the Department of Education. This code provides guidelines, rather than precise instructions – expecting each school to exercise professional judgement in assessing special needs requirements.

When your child starts primary school, she will be given 'baseline assessment' tests. These tests aim to highlight the special needs any child might possess, and enable the school to work with your child in an effective and appropriate manner. However, problems may be missed – within a class of over thirty children, quieter and more passive individuals may go relatively unnoticed. It is important not to assume that your child's teachers always know best. Listen to your child and work with the school in relieving her personal difficulties.

When in confrontation with a school, many parents can feel they lack both the confidence and the technical knowledge to state their child's case satisfactorily. If you feel that you need the assistance of an informed outsider, it is possible, by contacting your Local Education Authority, to gain the help of what is termed a 'Named Person'. It is the aim of the present government that, by 2002, all parents with children who are being assessed for a statement for special educational needs will be offered the support of an independent Named Person. A Named Person is an individual – either professional or from a voluntary organisation or parents group – who will serve as an independent adviser, offering support and counsel while your child's needs are formally assessed. Although at first it might seem peculiar to enlist the help of an individual you have never met, you will soon find that a Named Person can become an extremely useful friend and ally in the struggle to educate your child.

As well as offering the help of a Named Person, most LEAs will be pleased to provide a help-line number, or the assistance of either a Parent Partnership officer or someone from a Parent Liaison Service. This person will consider your child's problems individually, and attempt to ensure you are provided with all the relevant information and support for his or her particular difficulties.

Although a teacher may fail to notice every child's particular needs, most class teachers and Special Educational Needs Co-ordinators (SENCOs) are keen to enable all children to work and learn to their best ability. They may ask you how your child is behaving at home. Don't feel afraid or insulted by this question – an honest answer can explain or help define the reason for any child's reading difficulty. Children who seem happy and settled at home, yet behave in a troubled way at school, are often found to suffer from a specific learning difficulty – while those with recent home troubles frequently manifest them in a school environment. Another possible reason for your child's learning difficulties may be a superficially trivial matter troubling her at school – perhaps unhappy friendships, or a poor relationship with a particular member of staff. Discussing both home matters and any school difficulties with teaching staff can be the only way to isolate either a particular reading difficulty, or a specific cause for your child's lack of motivation.

Most important, though, discussion with your child is the only way in which you or a teacher will obtain precise knowledge of any particular problems. One of the greatest worries for any young child who finds she is unable to read easily is the fear that she is losing control of her life. The liberty to talk freely concerning her fears with a caring and considerate adult can immediately lead in some ways to a feeling that these personal and previously unexpressed fears are controllable.

The role of a SENCO is in part to assist you and the school in the identification of any child with particular special needs. Further to this, they are the principal implementers of the five stages. Communication between you and your SENCO is vital. Both within the Warnock Report, and the 1981 and 1988 Education Acts, considerable stress is placed upon achieving a successful relationship between teacher and parent. Indeed, the Educational Reform Act (1988) provides a central role to parents in making decisions about their children's education in many spheres – this extends to all pupils with special educational needs.

Following the Children Act (1990), this central role applies not simply to a child's natural parents, but also to step-parents and guardians. All individuals who have assumed what is known as parental responsibility for a child have a right to information regarding her welfare, and to express a view on any aspect of her school career. The one exception to these rights occurs when a parent or guardian is debarred by court order; this occurs only very rarely. Significantly, this can mean that more than two individuals are regarded as parents for any particular child.

It is important to note that both schools and LEAs are bound to consider the Code of Practice. Established in September 1994, this code provides considerable guidelines for special needs education. According to it, schools are legally obliged to state within their prospectus the name of the Special Educational Needs Co-ordinator, the school's arrangements for detailing and deciding which children require what stage of special needs, and their own plan for working closely with parents. But while individual teachers are obliged to note this code, they are not compelled stringently to obey its guidelines. The code – in which the five stages of special needs teaching are detailed – suggests levels at which any child with particular special needs should be placed. It is up to teachers, a child's SENCO, and the LEA to determine which child requires what level of education.

If your school has a caring and effective SENCO, appropriate assistance for your child should be relatively easy to obtain. Most children will, at some point in their school life, experience mild difficulties learning certain aspects of the school curriculum – finding particular tasks more difficult than their peers. Solving these mild problems should be regarded as a key element of good teaching. There will, though, be some for whom these learning difficulties persist for all, or a large proportion of, their school life. These individuals – possessed of mild learning difficulties – form by far the greatest proportion of all children with special needs.

In many cases children with mild learning difficulties can, with assistance, follow the normal curriculum successfully. Indeed, most should, with the appropriate support, be able to participate in ordinary classes. The logical initial steps of the programme for special reading tuition – labelled 'stage one' by the Code of Practice first established by Warnock – offer a considered evaluation of your child's capabilities and needs. During this first stage of discussion and assessment, you and your child's school will, hopefully, devise changes and strategies which will enable her to overcome personal reading difficulties. Every child's literacy problems will be effectively pin-pointed, and a learning scheme designed for those experiencing these difficulties applied. With stage one assistance, pupils are frequently able to remain in a normal school environment.

From September 1998, all children have been assessed as they commence primary school education. This assessment – termed 'baseline assessment' – aims to indicate as soon as possible which pupils require special needs education. Although some children inevitably and invariably slip through the net, this should mean that if your child has special educational needs they will be spotted more quickly than previously, and entered into stage one of special needs assistance. Even for parents with the confidence to work successfully with their child's teacher and school, it can be an embarrassment when confronted with official jargon. When informed, initially, that their child is entering into stage one of special needs assistance, many parents become immediately afraid that their child will be perpetually hallmarked as 'different' – unable to cope with a normal school environment. It is a common misconception that the term 'special educational needs' applies only to the two per cent of children possessed of severe educational difficulties. In fact, these difficulties range from the mild to the severe. In January 1997, schools stated that eighteen per cent of their pupils – 1.5 million children – had special educational needs. Many of these will not, obviously, be among the one-twelfth of children who leave school with no GCSEs. Most who undergo stage one assistance do so simply for teachers to acquire awareness of their particular personal needs. Extra attention at this early stage can frequently solve a child's reading problems.

The primary aim of stage one assistance is a detailing of any difficulties your child is experiencing, coupled with possible causes for these problems. As such, be prepared for the school to ask you personal questions, both about your child's current and previous health, and concerning his or her progress at school and in the home. Should the assistance that both you and the school's SENCO and staff offer at this time indicate that your child requires further help – or should your child initially be judged to suffer more severe learning difficulties – they will enter stage two of the assessment process.

Stage two of the programme is concerned with setting precise targets for your child's particular educational needs. This may involve your child being given extra help from a learning support teacher. It will also involve the creation of an Individual Education Plan (IEP); a scheme aimed at setting your child goals which are suited to his or her personal requirements. This plan aims to set and prioritise your child's current difficulties; it also serves to provide a specific outline of goals on which you should work with your child to achieve by particular dates. Each IEP will be specific to one pupil – however, the aims listed in an IEP are usually fairly general. An example of an aim frequently given might be to attempt to learn specific key words, or develop an understanding of letter and letter group sounds which will enable your child to relate them to the written word.

Hopefully, the specific and realistic targets demanded by your child's IEP will enable them to reach new levels both of learning and of confidence. It is particularly important that your child is provided with a plan which they feel they can, with encouragement and assistance, reach within the time limitations. Ideally, an awareness of your child's personal level, and an establishment of their IEP, will come about only with careful and precise work and discussion between you, their class teacher, and their SENCO. The school may ask you to work with your child at home – if this is the case, your personal assistance and any time and encouragement you can make available may prove a vital boost to their learning.

Many children are considerably assisted by the creation of a specific goal which they can reach. After suffering difficulties at school, confidence is improved by the knowledge that targets are attainable. It is important to maintain an equable balance between keeping your child's learning targets simple enough to master, and establishing a challenging and interesting role for her. If a child finds condescension rather than encouragement, this will inevitably hinder her progress.

A particular aid to any parent at this level in her child's education can be close study of her school's special educational needs policy. As a parent, you have an automatic right to examine this policy, and to receive a copy of the school's annual report, which will include an in-depth summary of that policy. Learning and understanding the precise nature of your child's school education, and in particular the special needs tuition it provides, is an essential element of maintaining an efficient balance and equanimity between school and home study.

Many children who reach stage two of special needs tuition find that, with encouragement, this meets their requirements sufficiently. All of the work done at stages one and two should be regarded as supplementary to your child's normal class work. Hopefully, no further special needs tuition will be required. However, at times, your child's problems will not be so easily solved. If any child exhibits persistent difficulties, she may be offered medical examination; it may also benefit a school if they are given permission by you to discuss the child's problems with her doctor. Ultimately, it may be concluded that your child needs to progress to stage three in order to obtain sufficient assistance.

Stage three generally involves calling in specialist help and advice; teachers and the SENCO will now be supported by professionals who specialise in the pupil's area of need. For ease of access, these needs are defined as referring to five areas – Behaviour Support, Learning Support, Non-teaching Support, Sensory Support and Specific Literacy Support.

In contrast to those children whose difficulties concern the majority of their curriculum, some individuals suffer problems in a more precise area of study. These specific learning difficulties can hinder all areas of study – for example, a child with difficulty in reading will be less able to learn than one with normal literacy levels. But children with specific learning difficulties can become extremely frustrated if the same processes of special needs tuition are applied to their particular difficulties. These children may, for example, have considerable trouble with literacy, yet show a clear and intelligent awareness of concepts in oral examination. Such a child will, inevitably, become frustrated by the low demands expected of one possessed of more general difficulties. The establishment of a precise programme is particularly important in such contexts.

Level three of the Special Needs Register generally indicates that your child's particular learning difficulties are sufficiently severe to hinder her access to and comprehension of the curriculum, whether through simple learning difficulties, or more specific problems with numeracy or with literacy. The school may well arrange for an educational psychologist to investigate your child's personal reading difficulties more thoroughly. It is at this stage that your child may well be determined as suffering from a specific learning difficulty.

Having considered your child's personal difficulties more precisely, it will probably be judged necessary to establish a new and more precise learning programme enabling her to progress as easily as possible. The school will monitor this programme carefully, while as a parent you will be encouraged to become involved in your child's educational welfare. This encouragement may take the form of regular invitation to review meetings.

Your child's teachers will be sure to take account of any specific learning difficulty, and it is important that both you and they employ the educational psychologist's advice to the full. Further assistance both to confidence and to learning may be provided by use of a dictaphone – enabling the child to remember class lessons effectively – and a computer. By making use of both spell-checking programs and computer-based learning packages, many children find they can make considerable progress. It may be possible, if you are particularly concerned with your child's progress, at this stage to enter into a written agreement with her school. Ask your local Parent Partnership group to assist you in the preparation of this document, which should serve as a form of contract detailing precisely the level of support both parents and school will offer to a particular child.

Teachers are, in general, becoming increasingly skilled at understanding and aiding a variety of specific learning difficulties. Indeed, one of the primary guidelines expressed in the 1997 Green Paper 'Excellence for all children' states that by the year 2002 'there will be national guidance on training governors to carry out their responsibilities for pupils with SEN'. With this increased awareness, many children are able to continue tuition in a mainstream school despite problems which can appear quite severe. The training now available to all teachers is not merely beneficial to pupils suffering dyslexia or other literacy problems; by utilising particular teaching strategies, a successful teacher can hope to boost the literacy of the class as a whole.

The educational psychologist's assessment at stage three should ensure that the cause of any specific learning difficulties is established. However, many parents find that an appointment with the psychologist is difficult to come by, and that when it is finally obtained the time offered is ultimately insufficient. This owes much to the absence of time and money, which permeates the special needs sector. Although LEAs, at the time of writing, spend one-seventh of their budget on special educational needs, the funding required for individual assessment is considerable. Coupled with this, current educational guidelines aim to educate children with special needs within the normal school curriculum as frequently as possible. As David Blunkett, the Secretary of State for Education and Employment, has observed in the Green Paper 'Excellence for all children', there is 'a strong reason for educating children with SEN, as far as possible, with their peers. Where all children are included as equal partners in the school community, the benefits are felt by all.'

The downside of this equal opportunities policy, however, can be that children whose needs are not well met by the school curriculum may find themselves hindered within that system. Nevertheless, most experts ultimately desire nothing but the best for your child, and will attempt to ensure that her progress is very carefully monitored.

Almost all children who require extra assessment and support find that assistance in the first three stages of the special needs programme enables them both to learn and regain confidence effectively. For approximately three per cent of all children, though, this level of support does not prove sufficient. These children progress to stage four. This level is in itself something of a limbo stage, at which a 'statutory assessment' of the child is required. This assessment serves to determine whether a child requires a Statement of Educational Need. The statement will outline the concerns about the individual pupil's circumstances, and should be supported by careful monitoring by your child's special needs teacher.

Your child's school may ask for her to be given a statutory assessment; it may also be asked for by a professional who is unrelated to teaching, such as your child's doctor. Whoever makes the request, it is important to remember that they must contact you, as a parent, before doing so. It is also possible for you personally to ask the LEA to make a statutory assessment of your child. But, just as any school or doctor will talk to you before making the request, you should always attempt to discuss the matter with your child's school before making this petition.

The LEA is allowed six weeks to inform you whether or not they have decided to make a statutory assessment of your child. Should the LEA decide to make a statement concerning your child, they are legally obliged both to tell you of their plans, and to assign you a particular staff member – sometimes termed your 'Named Person' – who will provide you with further information. Hopefully, the assessment should take place as part of a two-way process between you and your LEA, in which they ask for your personal views. You will be encouraged to tell the LEA your opinions on your child's difficulties; you will also have the right to accompany your child to any interview, medical test or other aspect of the statutory assessment. As a parent, it is important, too, that you strive to obtain your child's personal views on her learning difficulties. These views can hold profound weight in determining the result of a statutory assessment – understandably, however, many children are nervous about expressing their views in the company of strangers.

The LEA should explain clearly and lucidly what steps they intend to take, should your child be assessed. They are also obliged to provide up to twenty-nine days in which you are allowed to decide whether or not you wish your child to be assessed in the manner they have described. All parents must by law be allowed contact with their SENCO. Further to this – and in concordance with the Educational Reform Act of 1988 – any child with a statement of special needs must be as fully integrated into the normal activities of the school curriculum as possible.

Should the petition for further aid, and for a Statement of Educational Need, provide insufficient evidence that a child requires extra assistance, that child will return once more to stage three. If you are severely worried concerning your child's learning difficulties, it is essential that at this stage in particular you attempt to provide convincing evidence concerning those problems to your Local Education Authority. It is extremely expensive for your LEA to provide sufficient assessment to establish a Statement of Educational Need; many councils would understandably prefer to keep children isolated to the first three stages of the special needs programme. If you genuinely believe that your child requires more aid, your personal and assertive reasons for this view are particularly necessary at this time. Remember, however, that most teachers are on your side – the problem is not with the teaching profession, but with the lack of finance provided.

Usually, the SENCO will be the person who petitions the LEA for a statement for your child. However, if you feel you are not being provided with the co-operation you need from your child's school, it is possible to write directly to your

LEA. They should provide the addresses of people and organisations you can approach to obtain statutory help for your child. At the time of writing, the Department of Education offers a useful booklet called *Special Educational Needs – a guide for parents*. This booklet is simple, jargon-free and details various ways in which it is possible to seek extra help for your child within the state system. A further aid for parents bewildered by the system may be obtained from the local education department, who will be happy to provide both information and help-line numbers for parent link groups that can offer advice or support.

If you sincerely believe that your child's petition for assessment has been unjustly denied, it is possible to appeal to the Special Educational Needs Tribunal. Although most difficulties can be rectified by discussion with your child's school, or her Named Person, in some cases appeal to this Tribunal can seem the only way to enable your child to get the aid she has been unfairly denied. You can appeal to the Tribunal if the LEA refuse either to make a statutory assessment when asked by you, or to make a statement following their assessment. It is also possible to appeal if your LEA refuses to assess a previously assessed child again, or if your LEA decides to stop maintaining your child's statement.

Of course, the concept of taking something concerning your child's welfare to a Tribunal can inevitably seem overwhelming and deeply intimidating. If you require help in preparing your child's case, it is possible – and indeed advisable – to seek help from a number of sources. The Tribunal itself, voluntary organisations, parents' groups and, perhaps most important, your child's own Named Person can all provide help in preparing your child's case. It is also possible to ask up to two professionals who know your child to speak on your behalf at the Tribunal.

The Tribunal consists of three people. One, the chairman, will also be a lawyer; the remaining two will, between them, hold experience both of special educational needs and local government. Together they will consider the evidence and provide a final decision upon your child's problems. If your child's LEA has failed to follow the Code of Practice in the case of his or her learning difficulties, the Tribunal will require a detailed and thorough explanation of their reasoning. However, should the LEA provide legitimate reasons for their action, there is no reason why straying from the code should necessarily mean their actions were wrong.

If the petition proves successful, your child will move on to the fifth and final stage of the special needs programme. Stage five indicates that a child's difficulties have so affected access to the regular curriculum that the county has prepared a 'Statement of Educational Need' and has supplied extra support. A statement is initially prepared in draft form, in five sections:

1 *Personal Information*
2 *Special Educational Needs*
   The child's special needs are summarised and appropriate educational objectives are outlined.
3 *Special Educational Provision*
   The provision which the Education authority regards as appropriate for your child's special educational needs are outlined.
4 *Appropriate School or Other Arrangements*
   Here, the school to which the Education Authority proposes to send your child will be detailed. As we will see, their opinion is not necessarily final.
5 *Additional Non-educational Provision*
   In which are recorded any special provisions being made

for your child outside of school relating to her personal special needs.

This statement should clearly detail the particular needs of your child, coupled with a firm summary of the extra assistance it is believed she should be offered by your LEA. This help might come from within a school; it might also, if appropriate, require that your child is granted speech therapy, aid from hearing and visual handicap support services, or psychological support. Following the creation of the draft statement outlined above, you as a parent have fifteen days in which you are able to comment upon or detail disagreements with the statements and objectives outlined, either in written form or to an officer of the Education Authority. Following this, your changes are considered and a final statement is prepared. If you disagree with this final statement, it is still possible to petition your disagreements – first to a Local Appeal Committee and ultimately to the Secretary of State.

If your child has been granted a Statement of Educational Need by your LEA, the support it details as required should take effect immediately. It is important to note that, once your child has been granted a statement, it will remain with her regardless of whether she moves school or county. Wherever your child is educated, that school's governors will be obliged by law to provide the assistance detailed in her personal statement.

It is sometimes possible for a child to obtain education at an independent school, should it be judged that this system will provide effectively for the special requirements of that child. However, at the time of writing the LEA is free to choose a state school, should it judge this to be the best option, regardless of whether the parents or even the special needs teacher considers a child's interests would be most fulfilled in an independent school. You possess the right, however, to express a preference for any particular state school. The LEA must, generally, accept your choice – although this is cautiously qualified. Should an LEA judge the school you have chosen for your child to be unsuitable to her age, ability and needs, an ineffective use of LEA resources, or a hindrance to other children in that school, he or she will reject your requests. But although the LEA do make the final decision, they are legally obliged to inform you of their reasons and justification.

If a statement is made, an annual review will be maintained to ensure that your child's progress is as successful as possible. This review should alter your child's educational plan in concordance with her specific current needs. There are many reasons why your child might require the use of an educational plan, owing to either physical or neurological difficulties.

Should your child suffer severe difficulties, she may be exempted from aspects both of the curriculum and of curricular examinations. The principles guiding both examination exemption and special requirements for examinations are logically designed to remove, as far as possible, any disadvantages your child might endure owing to her specific difficulties. As such, these exemptions tread a fine line – neither hindering a child with difficulties, nor providing that individual with an unfair advantage over other pupils. If you feel that your child requires special arrangements for examinations, and these are not being taken into account, it is important to declare these convictions early. Individual candidates and their proposed special arrangements must be discussed with the Head of Examination Centre before the spring term of the year of their examinations. Establishment of special needs for a child may apply to course work as well as any examinations; it is important, then, to discuss your child's problems and consult the Regulations and Guidance issued by the examination authorities early on, and preferably before your child begins her course.

With the Green Paper 'Excellence for all children', the government expresses its intention considerably to diminish the sense of isolation that some children feel. As we have seen, this is intimately bound up with an interest in keeping children with special needs within the curriculum, unless special requirements demand or suggest that your child would benefit from particular non-curricular schooling. This system has considerable benefits; it is also particularly reliant upon helpful and efficient relationships between parents and the school system.

Within this book, it has been my aim to outline the specific forms of reading difficulties which might affect your child and how best to overcome them. These problems can range from the mild to the acute. However, most children, if aided in accordance with the guidelines which I have shown, will make good progress. Learning is intimately linked with confidence – which can be significantly increased by a careful realisation of the particular educational plan which will suit your child. By using the guidance found here, and by maintaining an effective and mutually beneficial relationship with your child's school, you will ensure that she is given the best possible education in accordance with her personal needs.

If your child is working within the state educational system, this may well mean that both you and she become involved in one or all of the stages of special educational need provision. The important thing is not to let the system faze and confuse you. In practice, it is far more humane and caring than it may appear in cold print. It is designed primarily to enable every child to receive the education that she needs and deserves. Hopefully, working with this book, if your child does need special attention of this kind you will no longer feel intimidated by the state system and will have the confidence to ensure that your child is given the excellent level of education which should be her right.

Attempt to establish which strategies and teaching methods aid your child most effectively. If you find a particular process is successful, tell her school. Similarly, learn from her teacher's own educational methods. I have stated that the principal driving force behind many reading difficulties is lack of confidence. This problem can only be solved by enabling your child to obtain an education which she finds both under-standable and inspiring. Within this book, I have aimed to provide guidelines which should enable you to make your child a better reader – both in your time and within the school system. Initial problems with literacy, however slight, inevitably lead to a lack of confidence and a spiral into further reading difficulties. The most effective way to fight this reaction against reading is by an intimate knowledge of your child's personal educational needs. Frequently, this may be enough to stop the spiral before it gets out of control.

Appendix

W – word search

w	h	a	t	b	z	r	v	w
n	q	w	h	i	l	e	w	h
w	a	v	w	k	w	z	k	e
h	z	y	x	h	e	w	h	r
e	d	u	c	f	r	u	w	e
n	s	i	a	m	e	z	k	k
t	h	b	b	p	f	w	h	o
w	a	v	x	z	t	l	p	s
d	x	w	h	y	o	u	y	r

Find these words and draw a ring around each one

were, what, when, where, which, while, who, why

Word search framework – photocopy and use to practise
the words you are working with

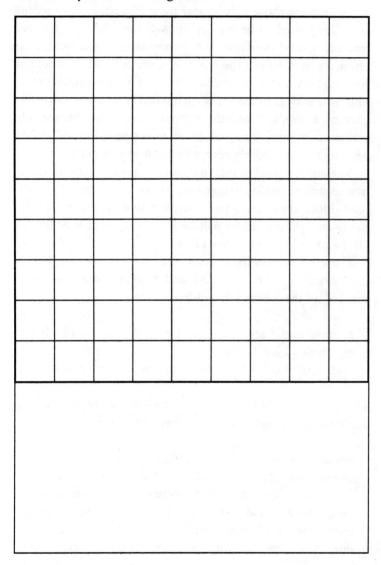

The first one hundred basic keywords

Keywords are those that appear most frequently in everyday text. They need to be learned so well that they can be read and recognised on sight. When you are reading with your child, try to point out the words you are currently learning or have just learned in his reading books. This is especially valuable as it will teach him how each word appears in context as part of a simple sentence. Keywords can also be usefully practised in word games as, to be ready easily on sight, they need to be immediately recognised out of context as well.

Just one hundred words make up on average half of all the non-technical books, magazines, letters and papers that you read. Once these are known so well that they can be read easily on sight the reader will be able to tackle at least half of all the print he comes across in an instant.

These thirty-two basic keywords are the most frequently used words in written English and account for around one-third of all the words you read:

a	all	and	are	as	at	be	but	for	had	have
he	him	his	I	in	is	it	not	of	on	one
said	so	that	the	they	to	was	we	with	you	

These words added to the thirty-two words written above make up about half of all your non-technical reading:

about	an	back	been	before	big	by	call
came	can	come	could	did	do	down	first
from	get	go	has	her	here	if	into	just	like
little	look	made	make	me	more	much	must
my	new	no	now	off	old	only	or	other
our	out	over	right	see	she	some	their	them

| then | there | this | two | up | want | well | went |
| were | what | when | where | which | who | will | your |

These words can be taught easily over time using word searches, word dominoes, word remembering games and word snakes and ladders. There are some grids over the page to help you make up your own word searches. Take a common-sense approach and start off small by learning two or three keywords with your child every week and playing games to practise them. Some children will want to move along quicker, some like to stay longer practising what they already know. Be guided by your child's reactions because as well as teaching him how to read basic keywords almost instinctively, you are helping to boost his confidence. You are helping him to understand that reading is just like riding a bike – when you start to try it seems almost impossible, then you listen and practise, and all of a sudden you realise that you can manage alone.

The following list comprises the next one hundred most commonly used words. Together with the first one hundred most frequently used words in English print they make up almost three-quarters of average reading material. There are a lot to learn and this may be a little daunting for children just starting to learn to read, so take teaching and learning at the pace they appear happiest with. Once they feel completely comfortable, move along, helping them to learn these words using the same types of word games you used before. Obviously, if your child enjoyed one type of game the most, play that more often than others. He will learn much quicker if he enjoys the game, learning by stealth is immensely valuable so use the words as part of a fun game rather than making a heavy point of hammering them home. Once a child has learned to read the one hundred basic keywords automatically on sight he will be feeling more confident about his reading ability so most children will be happy to try to learn four or five of these new words every week. If they are obviously trying, but finding learning at this speed a worry, back off and just introduce one or two new words into your games gradually whenever you play. They will be a novelty and as such more easily remembered. Always play the word games they want to play at the time, expect that you both concentrate and play by the rules, and have a good time.

The high-frequency words to be taught as 'sight recognition' words in years one and two under the Department of Education Literacy Strategy are mainly taken from these lists of the basic two hundred keywords used in all everyday text. But as well as these, children are taught to sight-read some other, perhaps more child-based, common words, like mum, dad, dog and play.

The Second hundred most used words

These words added to the one hundred words most used in written English make up almost three-quarters of all the non-technical text we read and write. Most reading schemes build up basic ability to sight-read common keywords by practising known words and by gradually introducing new ones into the text. Reading with your child will help him to become very familiar with all these words over time and making the time to share playing word games with him will make him even more confident. Colours, number names, days of the week and months of the year as well as these basic common words all need to be recognised and read automatically. Children learn most easily through play and can build up a rock-solid recognition of words if they see and use them frequently through games.

after   again   always   am   another   any   ask   away
bad   because   best   bird   black   blue   boy   bring
day   dog   don't   eat   every   far   fast   father   fell
find   five   fly   found   four   gave   girl   give   going
good   got   green   hand   have   head   help   home
house   how   jump   keep   know   last   left   let
live   long   man   many   may   men   mother   Mr
never   next   once   open   own   play   put   ran
read   red   room   round   run   sat   saw   say
school   should   sing   sit   soon   stop   take   tell
than   these   things   think   three   time   too   tree
under   us   very   walk   white   why   wish   work
would   year

When you read with your child you will find these words cropping up over and over again. Children love looking for and spotting a particular word or picture when they are reading or rereading a story. Try picking out one or two words every time you read with him and asking your child to point them out whenever he spots them in the story you are reading together. Looking for a special word makes it very memorable and focuses his attention into following every word on the page as you read it. Many children find this easier if you point to each word as you read it.

Tall and short letter clues

The shape of letters can give clues as to what they are. Some children love to puzzle out which word fits into the grid by working out how each individual letter should fit in. Sit with them and join in when they play this game, help them to read out the list of possible words and then give them a little time to think for themselves before you gently guide them with little obvious common-sense things to look for 'Do any of the words in the list start with a tall letter?' 'How many letters are there in this word?' 'Where do the tall letters need to go?' Remember to offer any help very subtly so that your child feels a real buzz at working things out for herself successfully.

all
as
and

at
are
as

at
be
but

for
had
have

he
him
I

his
in
it

not
is
of

on
one
said

so
that
the

they
to
was

we
with
you

Active basic keyword games

The problem with helping children who don't enjoy sitting and reading with you to learn how to sight-read words on their own is that most of the words that occur most frequently in written English mean little when they stand alone. It would be easy to write the word 'dog' under a picture of a border collie but it is very difficult to picture words like 'while', 'could' or 'what'. The secret is to play with a small group of words at a time, try to link them in some straightforward logical way and store the game so that you can play it again and again. One of the most useful sets of words you can practise are these common 'w' words all of which seem to cause problems for many children: Want, were, what, when, where, which, will, with, would.

Children are very often confused by so many of these common 'w' words and it is important to find enjoyable ways of helping them learn to distinguish one from another. When working with young children, don't try to teach them more than two or three words in a week. Write on big connecting bricks or empty individual cereal packets and label each with one letter from the target word:

w	a	n	t		w	h	i	c	h

Then help your child to stick the bricks or packets together in the correct spelling order. Always go over what you have learned the week before, keep on practising and move on slowly. Sticky labels can be used to mark each brick with the letter you want and this has the advantage that you can remove one and replace it with a different letter easily, but they do tend to look tatty after quite a short time. Writing letters on with marker pens or sticking on plastic letters produces a much smarter finish.

Once your child is obviously reasonably sure of each word get her to shut her eyes while you take away a letter; when she opens her eyes again she can work out what letter is missing. Let her choose a brick with the correct letter on it and put it back into the word. If you don't have a big set of packets or bricks already made up, let your child make her own by using a marker pen to write the letters he needs on a spare brick or packet. This is a good way of ensuring that she remembers every letter in the word she is playing with and this stops confusion between 'w' words both when reading and spelling.

More work with 'w' words

Connecting plastic bricks are a particularly good way of showing children how you can stick and the letter sounds that make up words. This is useful for teaching phonics as it shows children very clearly how each word is made up. I have found it an effective way of teaching children who have mild specific learning difficulties as it is practical and involves them in doing things rather than in learning by rote.

| Wh | e n | | w | i | ll | | wh | i | ch | | w | e | ll |

It is also a very clear way of helping children distinguish between words that look extremely similar and differ only by one letter. For instance, make up the word 'where', take away the 'h' and you have 'were'. (This also works well with 'through' and 'though', two words that seem to cause beginner readers endless confusion.)

Letting children discover and understand how words are made up by touching and building is often a very useful way of helping those who have specific language difficulties. They seem to feel more in control and I have found it a big help in teaching. Sadly, basic keywords are often difficult to spell phonetically in a straightforward way. Words like 'what', 'want', and 'when' sound, when many English people speak them, as 'wot', 'wont' and 'wen'. So the easiest way of teaching a child to read, remember and spell them is to use simple mnemonics:

w + hat   w + ant   w + hen

Young readers (and particularly young spellers) have great trouble working out the word 'would'. The key seems to be in remembering this silly, but it seems very memorable, mnemonic:

walk-o-u-lazy dog

For some reason children seem to remember this for ever.

Mnemonics; nifty ways of remembering how to read and spell some basic words

Readers and spellers tend to get confused by the same words every time and each tiny mistake chips away at their confidence. Try to help your child to learn these words by writing them down together alongside their mnemonics. Say them out loud while you are playing together and when you feel certain that they are in place ask your child to spell them. Being able to spell out a word that they have previously found difficult delights children and makes them realise how their hard work is helping them progress. Mnemonics tend to be trite and ridiculous, but these are all tried and tested ways of remembering quite difficult basic words and they will usually do the trick.

> because = big elephants always upset small elephants
> could = come o u lazy dog
> should = shout o u lazy dog
> school = some come hopping out of lessons (this is useful
> because many children are puzzled by the illogical
> placing of 'ch' in this word)
> round = run o u naughty dog
> around = always run o u naughty dog
> which = William Henry is coming home
> while = William Henry is looking East
> though = think o u good hen
> through = think right o u good hen

(In 'though' and 'through' children remember the sound 'th' better than separate 't' and 'h'.)

Mnemonics always look and sound silly but whenever your child struggles with reading or spelling any of these words help her to work it out by saying the mnemonic together and it will quite soon be firmly committed to her memory. If you find that your child has persistent difficulty remembering certain words, make up a mnemonic for that word together and write it down on a wall poster or in a small book. I have found that children who have a dyslexia problem find this a good way of remembering words that they have to read and spell frequently. Mnemonics work well but can obviously only be used to memorise a reasonably small number of words as there is a limit to how many mnemonics the average person can remember accurately.

Number words 1–10

1	one	6	six
2	two	7	seven
3	three	8	eight
4	four	9	nine
5	five	10	ten

Number puzzle sheet for numbers 1–10

This is a very simple puzzle for children just beginning to learn the relationship between numbers and their written names. Show your child how to draw a line between each number and its written equivalent.

1	three
2	one
3	two
4	six
5	five
6	four
7	six
8	seven
9	ten
10	eight

Make similar games for numbers 10–20 and upwards as needed.

A slightly harder number puzzle for 1–10

This puzzle is slightly harder because it involves looking further in order to match up numbers and words. Try working through it together with your child, looking up each number when you come across it on the basic number/word sheet. Photocopy or make up a similar sheet so that she can repeat the puzzle. Once they get the hang of it, many children like to use sheets like this when they are playing schools or just as something to do when they feel like a quiet activity. Doing puzzles when they are super certain of the answers may seem of little use but it builds confidence and will help them to link numbers and their written names automatically.

1	five
2	seven
3	six
4	eight
5	three
6	nine
7	one
8	ten
9	four
10	two

Colour words

Get some felt-tips and help your child to colour in the box next to the colour name in the appropriate colour. The more she wants to practise this the better, as being able to recognise and read colour and number words are important for many written games and activities.

red ☐

yellow ☐

blue ☐

green ☐

brown ☐

black ☐

white ☐

purple ☐

orange ☐

pink ☐

Colour games

Linking colours with their written names is comparatively easy because children are surrounded by colours and are very interested in them. If you have packs of different coloured drawing or sticky paper at home, write the name of the appropriate colour clearly in the corner of each sheet – this can be done without damaging the paper by writing on removable Post-It notes. If you have the patience you can also write the name of the colour of each felt-tip on strips of sticky label and fix each one to the relevant pen. Children learn colour names quickly when you do this because they seem automatically to look at the name label whenever they pick up a pen and the name/colour link sticks in their minds.

You can help to fix these links by asking easy questions in turn and 'reading out' the answer from the relevant colour pen. Start by asking each other really simple questions like 'What colour is grass?' or 'What colour is your T-shirt?'. Move into the sort of question that gets you both talking and thinking about how important colours are in your lives. Ask about favourite colours, what colour the sky is today – anything that involves your child and gets her actively thinking and learning.

If your child has a paintbox that is big and basic enough, try labelling each colour and playing the same sort of games extending it to take in what colours mix together to make a third colour: a very simple game but one that teaches both colour name recognition and how blue and yellow make green, yellow and red make orange, and red and blue, purple. Move this game on to helping your child work out how to add white to black and red to make grey and pink, and how to add white, or use more water, to make a lighter colour. Make a block of each colour on paper and label it. Most children are very quick at spotting quite subtle differences between colour tones and enjoy working out different shades of the same basic colour.

Many children like to use the colour/name chart and write the colour names in appropriate places on pictures. Start by cutting out pictures from magazines and comics that have fairly broad spaces of one basic colour because young children usually have big writing and get upset if they can't fit their writing into a restricted space. Making a colour scrap-book is easy and something that almost all children really enjoy doing. Look through old magazines and packets, cut out one-colour shapes, stick them into a scrap-book or on a big sheet of paper and label with the appropriate colour names.

Active colour and number word games

Many young children don't like to sit writing, colouring, painting and talking – they want to be running around doing more active things. These games are only minimally disruptive, cost little or nothing and can keep a child happily moving, sorting, stacking, learning and having a good time.

Sorting laundry is a trial for parents but seems to be the purest joy for some children. Start by labelling separate cardboard boxes red yellow green blue and help your child to sort her clothes into the 'right' boxes. Try the same game with brown black white orange purple pink and grey – obviously, if you have the space, you can try the lot at the same time. Be subtly selective and try to stick to one-colour items as multi-colour patterns will be confusing.

If your child is lucky enough to have her own room, line the colour-labelled boxes along one wall and try sorting soft toys or cars into the 'right' colour boxes. But if she has to share a bedroom she can get very upset if a brother or sister messes up the system so in this case is may be perhaps best not to attempt this.

Try clearing a space in your child's room (or use a higher cleared shelf downstairs if there are younger children in the house to consider) and label it clearly with the colour of the week. Try having a red week for example and then whenever your child finds a red toy, picture, tin or packet help her to add it to the red display. This game can be played with the very young, as well as with children of school age, and they learn to recognise all the colour words you use very clearly over time.

If you have less space to play in, try labelling mugs with individual colour names and help your child to sort buttons, counters or little squares of coloured paper. You can easily cut one-colour squares out of old magazine pictures and older children will enjoy doing this with you. The best way of playing this game with very young children is if you can find plastic beakers in plain colours which you can then label with their colour names. This will help your child to make an immediate link between, for example, a red beaker and the red label on it. You can play this game from play-school age up and your child will learn to read colour names on sight without her even noticing that she can do it.

Children who are starting to write like to write over or copy colour names you have written down in the 'right' colour crayon. Green over the word green, red over red, blue over blue, and this practises hand control as well as reading.

Older children often enjoy making colour books for younger ones in the family. Just make up a simple book and label each page spread with a colour name. Then your child can use her imagination and cut out pictures from comics or magazines, and stick them on the colour-appropriate pages. This is a good way to develop the basic colour scrap-book idea and it encourages children to think about what kind of things the child they are making the book for would like to see in it. Try to make your book out of reasonably big sheets of paper as children tend to find the results more spectacular and rewarding if they are large-scale.

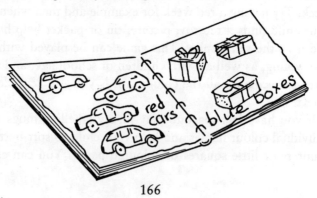

Plastic bricks are very useful for teaching basic spellings, especially colour and number words, to younger children. Collect six yellow bricks together and write one different letter from the word yellow on to each brick and build them up into a tower. Help your child to label up bricks and make a word tower for every colour you can manage, given the bricks available to you.

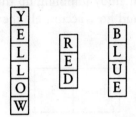

Boys, who are often less keen on sorting games than girls, are usually quite prepared to make a chart listing how many cars of differing colours they have stored away. Stick this list to their toy car storage box and they particularly enjoy updating it when they get a new toy vehicle.

My Cars			
red	yellow	blue	green

167

Number words

Teach number/number word links by writing a number on a label stuck to one plastic brick and labelling another brick of the same size with that number's written name. Then help your child to match them up and stick them together in pairs, ONE with 1, TWO with 2 and so on, as high as you both want to go. Older, more confident children enjoy jumbling up the labelled bricks and seeing how fast and how accurately they can match them up.

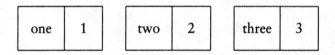

Little empty individual cereal packets make good number word skittles. Cover the front of each one with plain paper and write on the word for numbers up to ten. Take turns rolling a tennis ball across the room aiming it at the highest number word boxes. You score by reading out the numbers written on the boxes that you have knocked down and adding the numbers up on paper. The winner is the one with the highest score after each person has had two turns.

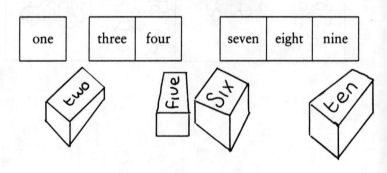

Number words can be practised by playing snap. Mark up one set of cards with numbers and another with the corresponding number names. One player has a shuffled hand of number cards, the other a shuffled hand of number name cards. Each player lays down one card as simultaneously as possible and if the name matches the opponent's number shouts 'snap'. Obviously, when playing with a beginner, try numbers 1–10 but this game can build up to larger numbers. It is useful for teaching the written names of 20, 30, 40 onwards and can be used for hundreds, thousands or millions if necessary.

Number words 10–20

Helping children to learn the relationship between these numbers and their written equivalent is more difficult than teaching those of numbers 1–10 because children have fewer everyday examples of them. The easiest way is still to draw the amount next to the appropriate number and word because this builds up a logical and visual link. Get a big blank sheet of paper and make up a poster with your child, work it out in pencil first because many children get upset and lose interest if they are half-way through a project like this and make a mistake in felt-tip, which is hard to remove and messy to alter.

11	eleven
12	twelve
13	thirteen
14	fourteen
15	fifteen
16	sixteen
17	seventeen
18	eighteen
19	nineteen
20	twenty

Number puzzle for numbers 10–20

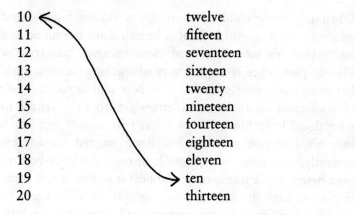

10	twelve
11	fifteen
12	seventeen
13	sixteen
14	twenty
15	nineteen
16	fourteen
17	eighteen
18	eleven
19	ten
20	thirteen

Names and addresses

Obviously every child needs to know his own name and address, and it is also helpful if he can learn the name and address of his school, and of close relatives and friends. Playing post office is a good way of teaching this. Save old letters and their envelopes that have been sent to you and talk to your child about how the letters get from the sender to your door. Help him to write a letter to himself and put it into an envelope that he has been assisted to address correctly, then either let him put it through the letter-box or, even better, put a stamp on it and post it so that it will come to him through the normal postal delivery. Children love to get something through the post so send them cards or little gifts, and encourage them to write or send drawings to other people.

When you are out walking show them the addresses written outside schools (particularly their own) and help them to read street names as they walk by. If their school sends out notes on headed paper cut off the heading and stick it on to plain paper so that your child can use it when he plays schools to write 'proper' letters home.

Learning the conventional layout and punctuation used in writing an address is very useful. Always help him to address letters and birthday cards, and at Christmas spend a little time in the weeks leading up to it addressing a few Christmas cards together every night. This will build up excitement and helps him to feel involved in the Christmas preparations. Save the front of birthday and Christmas cards and assist your child to use them as postcards to send to friends.

Encourage older children to send in entries to competitions in comics or on television and show them how to prepare a stamped, addressed envelope. Younger children are far more enthusiastic about writing and sending letters if they are sure of getting something in return, so encourage them to write to people who can reliably be expected to reply by return of post.

If you order goods from catalogues by mail let your child join in and help you to send off your order. As well as giving him practice of reading addresses it will give you an opportunity to explain how you send the money and how the goods you order get back to you. Young children often think that things arrive through the post from the post office down their road, so it is a good idea to show them on a simple map the part of the country that a particular letter or parcel has come from. If you have the time, talk about how it has got to you and how many people have been involved in its journey.

Names of months and days of the week

Most of the written names of months and days of the week are difficult to read and spell. Helping your child to write down the date in words every day and stick it up on the wall works well, but only if he enjoys doing it. If he is not keen to join in, write it up every day anyway in the kitchen or some other place where it is an obvious daily reminder to all the family and he will soon find himself looking at it and reading it every day.

❋ today is Monday September 25th ❋

Children who like writing, drawing and painting can usually be tempted to write out a verse or poem for their bedroom wall. Try the old favourite like Solomon Grundy or encourage them to make a weekly wall poster diary with broad headings for every day. This will give them constant practice of reading and remembering the days of the week, and will help to teach them how to organise their time. As children move upwards in school, being able to organise and prioritise their work and social time becomes increasingly important. If they learn the fundamentals of this basic organisation early it will be easier for them when they have far greater pressures on their time.

★ ❑ ■ ❈ ◈ ❙ ❈ Monday	take reading book and PE Kit to school
❈ Tuesday	Lisa coming here for tea
❈ Wednesday	go to Nan's house
❈ Thursday	Harvest festival at school
❈ Friday	roller skating 5p.m.
❈ Saturday	shopping with Mum
❈ Sunday	tidy up get things ready for school tomorrow

Names of Months

Names of months are even harder to learn to read and spell because there are more of them to remember. A daily calendar on the wall will help, but obviously it will take a full year before all the months come round. Most children like making a birthday poster for their bedroom walls to help them remember the birthdays of family and friends. This gives plenty of opportunity for your child to become familiar with the written names of all the different months because, as they make new friends, the poster will need constant updating.

January	Mum, Lisa
February	
March	Peter L. John
April	Nan
May	Uncle Andrew
June	Granny Pam, Lee Smith, Lucy R.
July	Grandad Bill
August	Jo, Ben
September	Jonathan
October	
November	Leslie
December	Helen M.

Reception year 'high-frequency' words

These are words that will be taught to your child in his first year at school as part of the National Literacy strategy. They are similar to the keyword lists and are all common words that children need to be able to read on sight to help them tackle their first reading books. Children will be learning and practising all these during their first year at school but they can of course also be incorporated into word games played at home.

I	to
up	come
look	day
we	the
like	dog
and	big
on	my
at	mum
for	no
he	dad
is	all
said	get
go	in
you	went
are	was
this	of
going	me
they	she
away	see
play	it
a	yes
am	can
cat	

Basic word bingo

This is a simple, easy game to help children learn to read and recognise words on sight outside the context of a story. As an example I have chosen words from the reception year list of high-frequency words on the previous page but you can of course adapt the idea to take in any words that your child needs to learn. Don't be over-ambitious; children can only cope enjoyably with a reasonably small number of words at a time. Write the words on the bingo cards being used (plus a few more words to make the game more interesting) on individual cards or small bits of paper and pop them in a box. For a two-player game take turns in taking out a word and reading it aloud, crossing it off your card if you find that word on it – as with most bingo games the first person with a line complete and crossed out is the winner.

Bingo Card for Player One

l	up	look	we	like	and
on	at	for	he	is	said
go	you	are	this	going	they
a	am	play	cat	to	come

Bingo Card for Player Two

day	the	dog	big	my	mum
no	dad	all	get	in	went
was	of	me	she	see	it
yes	can	an	as	be	by

Sight recognition words in years one and two

'Basic' words, 'keywords' and 'high-frequency' words are all terms meaning more or less the same thing – they are the words that occur most often in written English. These will all be taught to children when they are in year one or two at school. Some (like 'bed', 'school', and 'sister') are easy to learn because they can easily be linked with pictures but others need to be taught through games and repetition. Bingo works well, as does word dominoes or word snakes and ladders. Play with around twenty words at a time and use a mixture of words that your child knows on sight already combined with other words that he is as yet unsure of.

The problem with having set words that a child will be expected to know how to read on sight at a given time in his life is that all children are individuals and learn most readily in ways, and to some extent at times, best for them. Your child may not feel enthusiastic about reading in his first years in school and some can feel that they are falling behind because they have not learned to sight-read words that others in the class know. Don't get over-anxious if you notice that your child can't yet read words that others of his age recognise. Give him the opportunity to become familiar with them through reading and games, and to enjoy playing with words, and easy reading will almost certainly come when he feels ready for it.

about after again an another as back ball be
because bed been boy brother but by call called
came can't could did dig do don't door down first
from girl good got had half has have help her
here him his home house how if jump just last
laugh little live lived love made make man many

may more much must name new next night not
now off old once one or our out over people pull push
put ran saw school seen should sister so some take than
that their them then there these three time too took tree
two us very want water way were what when where who
will with would your

Word dominoes

This is more fun if you make word dominoes with your children rather than for them. If they don't immediately come up with words of their own help them to choose words that you notice they find tricky to learn (usual candidates are 'where', 'what', 'were', 'which', 'who', 'when', 'because', 'there', 'their', 'through', 'though', 'should', 'could' and 'would') and put one word either end of a strip of card. Use some of the words twice, in the same way that some numbers are duplicated on dominoes, share the dominoes between two or more players and enjoy the game.

should	could
should	
would	
would	through

Foul friends and nasty names

This is a game to help children get interested in using words in a way that adds fun to both their reading and their own writing. It is a big help to make out a list of words for children to choose from every time it is their turn to write down a description. Children generally much prefer this game if you give them a list of nasty adjectives rather than dwelling on virtues.

Choose a target person – friend, family or, even better, someone they hate and take it in turns to write a describing word.

For example start off with something like, 'Luke is slimy'. Then turn the top of the paper over and pass it to the child you are playing with so that she can choose a secret word from the describing list to add to it, let her write down her chosen word and pass it back to you. When the sheet of paper is full up, help her to unwind it and read out the whole demonic description of her chosen victim. This can be a helpful game to play with a child who you sense feels bullied or threatened by someone. Once you work out a description of that person together, laughter will have taken away much of the perceived bully's ability to frighten.

Work out words along these lines:

bad, blobby, bubbly, crawly, creepy, dismal, drippy, dull, dusty, fishy, foul, ghostly, ghoulish, grim, hideous, icy, jammy, jumpy, lumpy, messy, mouldy, nasty, naughty, noxious, peculiar, pongy, putrid, rancid, ratty, silly, slobby, smelly, strange, stringy, terrible, venomous, weird, wobbly

Try writing out a list together. Children love to learn and use new words, and really enjoy making them up for themselves, especially if they have someone close to bounce their ideas off. They will particularly relish being insulting about family, friends and enemies but are equally keen to hear good things about themselves, especially when they can laugh at the ridiculousness of it all. So try playing this game using over-the-top flattery.

Lisa is:

beautiful, brilliant, creative, delightful, excellent,
fantastic, good, heavenly, incredible, lovely, magnificent,
majestic, marvellous, queenly, radiant, supersonic,
terrific, unbelievable, wonderful

You will be able to think up more every time you play.

Word snakes and ladders

The easiest way of making this game is to buy a snakes and ladders board from a jumble sale and to stick a different commonly used word to each square. Alternatively, you and your child can make up a word snakes and ladders game together on a big sheet of paper or card. This example uses basic common words but this is also a good game for getting more familiar with number words, days of the week and months of the year. You play the game much as you do conventional snakes and ladders but the players read out the word they land on. The person to finish exactly on the last word (end) is the winner.

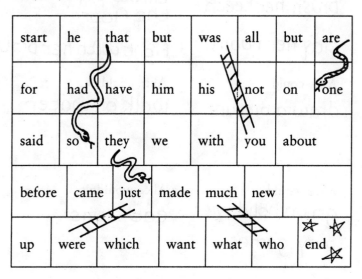

start	he	that	but	was	all	but	are
for	had	have	him	his	not	on	one
said	so	they	we	with	you	about	
before	came	just	made	much	new		
up	were	which	want	what	who	end	

Should, could, would and shouldn't, couldn't, wouldn't

These words confuse most children as they are difficult to both read and spell. The one good thing about them from a teaching point of view is that they can be practised very simply by making opposites lists. Sit with your child and draw up a simple two-column chart. This example uses the name Alice but when you are helping your own child to make up a list obviously substitute her name or the name of one of her friends or pets.

Alice should	Alice shouldn't
brush her teeth	throw paper on the floor
tidy her room	fight with her brother

Alice could	Alice couldn't
draw a picture	walk on water

Alice would	Alice wouldn't
go on holiday	eat slugs
play games	

This idea can be adapted very easily to help with learning will/won't, can/can't, shall/shan't and is/isn't.

Phonics and Phonemes

Phonics can come encased in mystifying jargon but all these unfamiliar words stand for some of the simple familiar sounds represented in your everyday reading by single and small groups of letters. It is merely the relationship between the letters on the page and the meaning and sound of words, the 's' sound and the letter 's' or 'ch', and the sound at the beginning of chocolate or cheese. Unfortunately English is far from a logical language and the relationship between sounds and letters is not always very straightforward. Some everyday words like 'eye', 'sigh', 'try' and 'pie' can't be worked from basic phonics. Many children are worried and puzzled by words like 'which', 'where', 'why', 'what', 'who', 'when', 'whose', 'their', 'there', 'enough' and 'people' which are basic to many of the books they read. These 'illogical' words need to be learned through familiarity within games and stories.

Phonics aren't magic but understanding the sounds that letters make can give children good clues to working out what the word they are puzzling over should sound like and this helps to give them confidence in their own ability to read for themselves. You almost certainly know all about phonics already but are simply unsure of the labels. Remember when you are helping your child that local accents can make the phonics of a written word confusing. Many of the children I work with are really bothered because they can't see the relationship between the sound of words they use all the time like 'anyfing', 'fick' and 'bruvver', and those that obviously mean the same thing that they see written in books. The simplest way of tackling this is just to teach 'anything', 'thick' and 'brother' as 'illogical' words that need to be learned by sight.

Phoneme
This is the smallest unit of sound in a word represented by one or more letters. There are around forty-four distinct phonemes in the English language.

Grapheme
This is the written representation of a phoneme.

Single Sounds
These are the first sounds that children are introduced to. The 'b' (ber) for bat and 's' (s) for Sam alphabet book sounds at the beginning of words. A good way of helping your child to feel confident using these is to run through the alphabet as a spoken or written word game, maybe trying to find the name of a friend that begins with each consecutive letter, A for Annie, B for Ben, C for Connor, D for David. Children all love this as it gives them a chance to talk about the friends they know at school and at home with their families, and they get very involved.

Short vowels
These are just the normal a,e,i,o,u, but are called short vowels simply because they make a short sound when they are spoken (comparable to the one they make in the normal-sound alphabet) when they appear in words. Cat, bat and match all have the short vowel 'a' in them.

Long vowels
Again these are just a,e,i,o,u but this time they make the longer 'proper letter name' sound within a word. A good tip to point out to the child you are reading with is that when a word contains a,e,i,o, or u followed by a consonant and ending in an 'e' then the middle vowel sounds like its letter

name. This isn't as tricky as it seems: words like 'make', 'take', 'fate', 'late', 'fade', all follow this rule. Sometimes the effect that 'e' after a consonant after a vowel has is referred to as 'magic e' – the classic examples of this is mat (here 'a' is a short-vowel 'alphabet sound') add 'magic e' after a vowel and a consonant, and it becomes mate (long-vowel 'a' as a 'proper letter name' sound). Some children get this at once and find it a real help but some are flummoxed by it. If this is the case don't labour the point or they will lose interest.

Blends
From single sounds children move on to the blends. Common consonant blends are sp, st, sl, sc, sk, tr, br, cr, fr, pr, sl, bl, cl, fl, gl, pl. Simple word games for practising these are seeing how many words you can find with one particular blend like 'spade', 'spin', 'spot', 'space'. Another good written word game is to pick out a common word ending like 'ay' and see if you can use various letter blends to make up a real word like 'st+ay', 'tr+ay', 'pr+ay' and 'pl+ay'.

Clusters
The sound made by a group of usually three letters like str or spr. A simple written rhyme game can teach these easily. Just make up a silly verse with your child along the lines of 'in the spring, we play with string' or 'Never catch a lighted match'. Try matching up beginning and ending phonemes: 'str+ike', 'str+oke', 'str+ay' or 'str+ap'. This is a good word game to play for five minutes or so but it needs to be tackled lightly to prevent it becoming tedious.

Consonant Diagraphs
The blend of two consonants usually at the beginning or end of a word. Sh, ch, th, wh and ck are all common consonant

diagraphs. A lot of the words that will make up your child's day-to-day reading begin or end with a consonant diagraph. Children seem to have very little difficulty remembering 'sh for shop' and 'ch for chocolate' but 'th for this' and 'wh for where' take far more time to become familiar. Children find learning the phonic sounds at the beginning of words easier than becoming confident with sound blends like ck that normally occur at the end of a word. The easiest word for most children to remember ending in ck is 'Jack', especially if it's their own name, or they know the rhyme 'Jack and Jill'. Try using words like 'back', 'black', 'sack' and 'pack' that rhyme with Jack to make up a story rhyme with your child.

Vowel+consonant diagraphs
A sound blend of two letters, one of which is a vowel and one a consonant. Ay, oy, ar, er, or, ir, ur, aw, ew and ow are all much used vowel+consonant diagraphs, which usually come in the middle or at the end of words. Use Lego bricks with single-sound letters on one and vowel+consonant diagraphs on the other to play at making up words and taking them apart again. 'S+ay', 's+aw', 'b+oy', 'b+ar' – just put the sounds together and see if they make a word that you and/or your child recognise.

Vowel diagraphs
Two vowels together that produce a phoneme, ee, ea, ai, ae, ie, oa, oo, ai are all vowel diagraphs. These can be learned and practised through rhymes. Make up verses together and point out the letter sounds that match. Try 'b-oo-t', 'f-oo-t', 's-oo-t', or 'm-ea-t' and 's-ea-t'.

Silent letters
These are the same old words containing seemingly soundless

letters that puzzled you at school. 'Gnaw', 'comb', 'know', 'knew', 'knuckle', 'gnat' and 'crumb' are the ones most used. When you are with your child and you come across a word with a silent letter, for example if you are out together buying gnaw sticks for your hamster, point out the silent-letter word as an oddity, sounding it out so that she sees that one letter seems completely 'invisible'. Some children are captivated by the strangeness of silent-letter words and always spell them faultlessly, others find them a mystery that they would rather avoid.

Within the National Literacy strategy children will be taught to recognise initial sounds (the first letter/sound of a word) a-z, ch, sh and th in their reception year.

During year one they will learn the middle vowel sounds (p-i-g, c-a-t) and learn to discriminate between the consonant blends and clusters: bl, br, cl, dr, dw, fl, fr, gl, gr, pl, pr, sc, scr, sk, sl, sm, sn, sp, spl, spr, squ, st, str, sw, tr, tw, hr, shr, id, nd, lk, nk, sk, lp, mp, sp, ct, ft, lt, nt, pt, st, xt, if, nch, lth, as well as ee, ea, ai, a-e, ay, ie, igh, y, oa, o-e, ow, oo, u-e, ew and ue.

In year two they will practise and build on the phonemes they have already learned and add to their knowledge by learning oo, u, ar, oy, oi, ow, ou, air, are, ere, ear, or, oor, aw, au, ore, er, ir, ur, ear and ea.

This list of the specific phonemes that your young child will be expected to learn sounds fearsome but most will be practised by reading and learning from stories, and children often learn phonics almost without noticing.

191

Basic phonics word games

Learning to read and spell words is helped along happily by playing with rhyme. I find large linking plastic bricks ideal for this as by writing for example 'r' on one brick and 'at' on another children can stick them together to make the word 'rat' and unstick them again to have another look at the sounds they have linked to make that word. Picking out words that rhyme together is a good way of checking that children can hear and recognise the often quite subtle distinction between the different sounds at the end of words.

Write 'b' on one brick and 'at' on another to make 'bat', 'c+ap', 'c+at', 'm+ap', 'p+at', 't+ap', 'm+at', 'l+ap', then group together the sets of bricks that rhyme.

m	ap
t	ap
l	ap
c	ap

p	at
m	at
c	at
s	at

Try making up very basic verses together with your child that use simple words that rhyme and write them clearly in a small book or put them on a sheet of paper on the wall:

My black cat	I have a tap
Has a black mat	and a yellow cap
and a flat hat	and a map on my lap

Or write down a word ending in a phoneme like ap, op, or ut and write all the words you can think of that end and rhyme in the same way:

cap	shop	hut
lap	hop	shut
snap	pop	but
map	cop	nut

These are just the simplest type of example and you can obviously make far more sophisticated rhymes. Dr Seuss books are a wonderful help in learning to read partly because they teach the rhyming similarity between words so cheerfully and well. Your child is almost certain to enjoy working out rhymes and stories together with you that you can make up into read-again books.

Phonic bricks

Plastic interlocking bricks are a great way to teach phonics and they appeal to both boys and girls. I make up several sets where each brick has a different phoneme (single and combination letter sounds) written on it in permanent marker and use them both to teach basic phonics and to construct and break down new words. With very young children, start with single letters and simple word endings, and just play with your child making up words and rhymes. They enjoy making words about things they know like 'dog' or 'cat', and they also learn a lot from making up words they find in reading books.

d	og		c	at		Sp	ot

Older children cope easily with smaller bricks and can use them by themselves to build up words and then put those words into sentences. As well as making up sets of bricks marked with different phonemes I also write keywords on them to enable children to build up simple sentences. If your child is having trouble with longer words show her how to make up that word from phoneme bricks linked together. Always encourage her to take apart the words you have made together and work out how to stick them back in the right order.

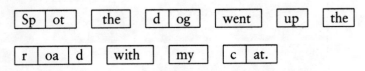

Once your child has started school she will be taught phonemes every week and will need your help both to learn and become totally familiar with them. I have always found that making up interlocking phonic bricks works very quickly and easily. For example, if your child is learning the consonant diagraph ch you just need to mark one brick with ch and make up other bricks with phonemes that could combine with ch to make up useful words:

ch	op		ch	in		ch	ur	ch		ch	at

Phonemes in the middle of words
Phonics is a dull thing to learn and to some extent to teach but it is obviously essential. Both boys and girls like using phonic bricks and learn more from taking apart a word and sticking it back together again than they ever would from just learning phonic words from a list. Children will make up and take apart each word quite cheerfully over and over again, and they remember both how to read and how to spell it. I have found that this method will adapt to help teach all words that can be made up with straightforward phonics. It is particularly useful to help children to understand the relationship between sounds at the beginning, middle and end of words:

b	ea	ch		b	un	ch		st	oo	d

When you are playing with rhyme, stick two bricks together to make a word ending like 'each' and try putting other letters on the front until you come up with a word that rhymes like 'beach', 'peach' or 'teach'.

Phonemes such as oa or ea are hard to learn and confusing for young children who have just been told that the individual letters within the combination both also hold their own phoneme. They understand the logic of making up words like 'c-a-t' by building up single-letter sounds but words like 'clean' and 'roam' don't make the same kind of sense. Mark a brick, packet or card with the combination phoneme you are practising and play at making words with your child by trying different letters before and after that sound. To practise oa, for example, try 'b+oa+t', 't+oa+st', 'fl+oa+t'.

This is a very simple, mundane game but it encourages children to experiment for themselves and write down the words that they work out. Obviously, poetry doesn't have to involve rhyme, but the more children learn how to make up, use and play with words the keener they are to create poems of their own. Some children take to writing stories and poetry from a very young age but others can get very tense if they are asked to write down their thoughts and ideas. Helping them to feel familiar with words and in control of what they are trying to write gives them the confidence to let their imagination run free.

| b | ea | n | | c | l | ea | n | | m | ea | n | | l | ea | n |

Doing words

Children all learn that verbs are 'doing' words but as well as describing understandable actions they often also involve tenses, something that frequently puzzles new readers and spellers. Teach the basic action first. Make up a pile of cards with one action ('walk', 'hop', 'smile', 'grin', 'run' etc.) on it and read them through with your child, then shuffle the cards and put them face down in a pile. The first player picks up a card, carries out the action written on it and the other player has to guess. After the word is guessed put it face up on the table so that everyone playing can check that it is right. This is a very simple game but children love doing the actions and get very involved.

Try cutting out pictures of people and animals from magazines and comics, and sticking them in a scrap-book with a suitable caption. Just something simple like: 'This dog is eating', or 'This man is sneezing'. Very young children like making these with you to read themselves and older children are often willing to make up scrap-books or write and illustrate similar posters and books for younger friends and relatives. Children frequently find the tenses of verbs difficult to master: 'I can walk', 'We walked', 'We were walking' are simple but many children are worried about when to use each word. Talk this out with your children and practise short sentences about things you do together. For example: 'I can walk to school', 'We walked to school yesterday', 'Luke and Emma are walking to school today', and look for examples when you read together.

A particularly good way of encouraging older children to try trickier variations of verbs is getting them to help by labelling photo albums with fairly full descriptions of what was happening when the photo was taken. Start by doing a few yourself to set the style, then ask them to take over. For example, they could label a beach holiday photo with something like: 'Here is a photo of me jumping on the beach at Brighton'. Just by labelling one set of holiday photos they can learn to recognise, read and spell verbs that they usually struggle over and try to avoid using when they are writing in school. Always give them easy access to a simple dictionary and stay near so that you can supply any spellings they need as and when they want them.

People, places and things

When your children are very young and just becoming aware of written words, label one or two things in their rooms like their beds and toy boxes, and talk to them about the relationship between the real thing and the written word that represents it. If they enjoy this you can label things around the house as and when it seems like a good time for you and them. If you have quite a lot of things labelled in a room, try writing each one on a card and putting it in a box, every player has to pick out a card, read it, then go and touch that particular object. This game can go on for years as you make each thing more obscure and difficult to find. Play at giving older children a list of tiny things to bring back, like a pencil, a toy car, a tin of beans, anything to get them reading and looking.

If you are someone who goes out shopping with a clear list of what you are going to buy (and sticks to it) let your child help you to check off each thing as you unpack it at home. Older children can help you write lists and can also often be persuaded to look up words in a simple dictionary and label things around the house to help younger brothers or sisters. The scrap-book idea is again useful: cut out things from catalogues, comics and magazines, and label them, in alphabetical order if possible. Make this together with very young children for their own use or ask older children to make up books and posters for younger ones.

Older children like making out fantasy wish lists. Sit with them and go through a shopping catalogue writing down all the things you would both buy if you won a thousand pounds. Most find this really absorbing and it helps reading, spelling, writing and basic maths.

Reading, spelling and grammar are obviously very much

interlinked and it is helpful for children to understand why some words have capital letters in print and others don't. Explain about the convention of always having a capital letter at the beginning of a sentence and also explain about proper nouns, the people, places and products that are always written with a capital letter. Point out shop names when you are out walking and brand names on clothes, food and drink. Look at names and addresses, and always look out for examples of how and why capital letters are being used when you read together. Some children will be curious enough to ask why capital letters are used to front some words but not others even before they start reading for themselves. Others seem not to notice and you will need to introduce the idea gradually as you read together.

Useful books and CD Roms

Books

The first rule of helping children get into reading is to let them have books they are really attracted to about subjects that interest them. Some children will read the labels on sauce bottles but others need to be enticed into reading by being strongly drawn to a particular book. The quality of books for young children is extremely high and your local children's library will help you and your child to find something that you both want to read and enjoy together. New books are being produced all the time so go along and see what you can find. Bookshops are no longer the straight-faced places they used to be and, for sensible commercial reasons, even the biggest bookshop chains are now very child friendly and will happily give you and your child a good chance to look through their children's book section before you buy.

Older children like to buy their own books but those who don't particularly like reading won't thank you for a book token when they were hoping for money to buy the sort of present they really want at the time. Much better to take them into a bookshop when you are out shopping and offer to get them a reasonably cheap book that they want as an extra treat. Discount bookshops offer good bargains and there is always a hope that a book-loving friend will go along with them and encourage them to join a library.

Here are some reading schemes for children just getting into reading. Despite their unfashionability, some children who find reading an unattractive struggle flourish on reading schemes. Whatever your views, if a child becomes captivated by 'Puddle Lane' or even 'Janet and John', she will be learning to love reading even if it is not in the free way that many parents would ideally wish for.

202

'Janet and John' published by: James Nesbit and Co., Digswell Place, Welwyn, Hertfordshire
'Puddle Lane' published by: Ladybird Books, Loughborough, Leicestershire
'Story Chest' published by: Thomas Nelson and Sons Ltd, Nelson House, Mayfield Road, Walton-on-Thames, Surrey. Story chest offers a huge number of big books and smaller readers. Thomas Nelson also produce a series called 'Flying Boot' which is good for young readers and older children who are only just starting to read for themselves.
'123 and Away' published by: Granada Publishing, PO Box 9, 24 Frogmore, St Albans, Herts
'Ginn 360' published by: Ginn and Company, Prebedal House, Parson's Fee, Aylesbury, Buckinghamshire
'Oxford Reading Tree' published by: Oxford University Press, Walton Street, Oxford

Children 7–9 who find reading a slight struggle often warm, to:

'Wellington Square' published by: Macmillan Educational, Houndmills, Basingstoke, Hampshire
'Fuzz Buzz' published by: Oxford University Press, Walton Street, Oxford

Older children and teenagers who find reading a struggle are embarrassed by being offered 'baby books'. These publishers offer books with age-appropriate stories that look right, the reading level is simple but they are popular with able and not so able readers alike:

'Quest Game Books' published by: Oxford University

Press, Walton Street, Oxford
'Hi-Lo Books' (reading level 7, interest level 9), 'Double Fastbacks' (reading level 8, interest level 11), 'Meanreads' (reading level 9, interest level 11+), 'High Stakes Adventures' (reading level 7, interest level 10) are just a few of the excellent series of books produced for older children and teenagers with little experience of reading. They are all published by: L. D. A., Duke Street, Wisbech, Cambridgeshire
'Hodder Real Lives' published by: Hodder and Stoughton, 338 Euston Road, London NW1 3BH

Both older and younger children enjoy joining in reading plays but very few easy-reading plays seem to be available in bookshops. Schools often have sets and may possibly lend you a copy.

CD Roms

Older children in particular often like to practise reading on screen rather than settle down with a book. Dorling Kindersley produce excellent CD Roms that children invariably seem to love. Younger children enjoy *P. B. Bear's Birthday Party* and *My Incredible Amazing Dictionary.* Those aged 8–16 go for *The Way Things Work* and *Stowaway.* For further information contact Dorling Kindersley, 9 Henrietta Street, Covent Garden, London.

New CD Roms designed to help children enjoy reading are being produced so fast that it is difficult to keep up with the progress that is being made. Ask your child's school and your local stores to see what is currently available.

Helpful Addresses

For further help and information about specific learning difficulties contact:

British Dyslexia Association
98 London Road
Reading, Berkshire RG1 5AU
Help-line 01189 668271
   The BDA publishes a wide range of information designed to help children and adults, and also offers a helpful befriender service.

Adult Dyslexia Organisation
336 Brixton Road
London SW9 7AA
Help-line 0171 924 9559
   Offers a range of educational services, information and support groups.

The Dyslexia Institute
133 Gresham Road
Staines, Middx TW18 2AJ
01784 463 851
   An educational charity specialising in teaching, assessment, training and advice.

National Association for Special Educational Needs
NASEN House
4–5 Amber Business Village
Amber Close
Amington
Tamworth, Staffordshire B77 4RP
01827 311 500
A very user-friendly organisation which offers accessible information aimed at encouraging the development of children with special educational needs and supporting parents.

Reach
Wellington House
Wellington Road
Wokingham, Berkshire RG40 2AG
Advice on resources – also compiles topic book lists for children with reading difficulties.

For parents reading with young children:

Bookstart
Books for Babies
Young Book Trust
0181 516 2984
For information and advice on reading with babies and very young children.

Basic Skills Agency
Commonwealth House
1–19 New Oxford Street
London WC1A 1NU
0171 405 4017
Produces an excellent magazine called *Read and Write*

Together designed to help parents reading and writing with children aged 3–5.

CEDC
Woodway Park School
Wigston Road
Coventry CV2 2RH
01203 655700
Resources for parents and children reading and writing together.

Contact your local library for information about children's library services and events. Many libraries hold story reading and telling sessions especially suitable for younger children.

If you are interested in volunteering to help with reading in a primary school, either contact your own child's school or:

VRH
Room 438
High Holborn House
49–51 Bedford Row
London WC1V 6RL
0171 404 6204
Train volunteers to give individual help to children having difficulties in learning to read.

For those working with older children and teenagers:

Boyz Own
Books for Students
Bird Road
Heathcote, Warwick CV34 6TB
01926 436 436

Produces a list of books designed to be particularly attractive and helpful for boys who are reluctant or less able readers.

British Dyslexia Association
98 London Road
Reading, Berkshire RG1 5AU
01189 668271
For information on useful books for children with dyslexia-related reading problems.

Reach
Resources for Children with Reading Difficulties
Wellington House
Wellington Road
Wokingham, Berkshire RG40 2AG
0118 989 1101
Produces helpful book lists for children and young people with reading difficulties.

Basic Skills Agency
Commonwealth House
1–19 New Oxford Street
London WC1A 1NU
0171 405 4017
Publishes a good range of materials designed primarily to help adults to improve their reading and writing skills. Many of the books it produces area also suitable for teenagers.

DFE Publications Centre
PO Box 2193
London E15 2EU
For many useful publications.

Bibliography

Adams, M. J., *Beginning to Read* (MIT Press, 1990)

Bryant, P. and Bradley, L., *Children's Reading Problems* (Blackwell, Oxford)

Clay, Dame Marie, *The Early Detection of Reading Difficulties* (Heinemann, New Zealand, 1985)

Clay, Dame Marie, *Reading Recovery – A Guidebook for Teachers in Training* (Heinemann, New Zealand, 1993)

Critchley, Macdonald, *The Dyslexic Child* (Heinemann, London, 1970)

Department of Education and Employment, *Excellence For All Children* (Stationery Office, October 1997)

Department of Education and Employment, *The Implementation of the National Literacy Strategy* (Stationery Office, 1997)

Department of Education and Employment, *Special Educational Needs – a guide for parents* (DFE Publications Centre, 1994)

Goswami, U. and Bryant, P., *Phonological Skills and Learning to Read* (Laurence Erlbaum Associates, 1990)

Hornsby, Dr Beve, *Alpha to Omega* (Heinemann, London, 1980)

211

Office for Standards in Education, *Reading Recovery in New Zealand* (Stationery Office, 1993)
Rosenthal, D. and Jacobson, A., *Pygmalion in the Classroom* (Holt, New York, 1968)

Index